Letter Links

Additional Resources Available From High/Scope Press

GENERAL READING RESOURCES

How Young Children Learn to Read in High/Scope Programs: A Series of Position Papers

Children Achieving: Best Practices in Early Literacy
S. B Neuman & K. A. Roskos

Beginning Reading and Writing
D. S. Strickland & L. M. Morrow

Facilitating Preschool Literacy
R. Campbell

Learning to Read and Write: Developmentally Appropriate Practices for Young Children
S. Neuman, C. Copple, & S. Bredekamp

Much More than the ABCs: The Early Stages of Reading and Writing
J. Schickedanz

Starting Out Right: A Guide to Promoting Children's Reading Success
M. S. Burns & P. Griffen

PRESCHOOL READING

Educating Young Children: Active Learning Practices for Preschool and Child Care Programs (2nd Ed.)
M. Hohmann & D. P. Weikart

Fee, Fie, Phonemic Awareness—130 Prereading Activities for Preschoolers
M. Hohmann

High/Scope Preschool Key Experiences Series: Language and Literacy Video and Booklet

Helping Your Preschool Child Become a Reader: Ideas for Parents

You and Your Child Parent Newsletter Series
12 titles: Young Children and Reading, Young Children and Writing, Young Children and Mathematics, Young Children and Art, Young Children and Dramatic Play, Young Children and Music, Young Children and Movement, Young Children as Family Members, Young Children as Communicators, Young Children as Decision Makers, Young Children as Challengers, and Young Children as Problem Solvers.

ELEMENTARY READING

High/Scope K–3 Curriculum Series: Language & Literacy
J. Maehr

Literature-Based Workshops for Language Arts—Ideas for Active Learning, Grades K–2
K. Morrison, T. Dittrich, & J. Claridge

Literature-Based Workshops for Mathematics—Ideas for Active Learning, Grades K–2
K. Morrison, T. Dittrich, & J. Claridge

Available from

HIGH/SCOPE® PRESS

A division of the High/Scope Educational Research Foundation
600 North River Street
Ypsilanti, MI 48198-2898
800/407-7377, FAX 800/442-4329
E-mail: *press@highscope.org*
Web site: *www.highscope.org*

Letter Links

Alphabet Learning With Children's Names

Andrea DeBruin-Parecki

Mary Hohmann

High/Scope Early Childhood Reading Institute

Ypsilanti, Michigan

Published by

HIGH/SCOPE® PRESS
A division of the High/Scope Educational Research Foundation
600 North River Street
Ypsilanti, Michigan 48198-2898
(734) 485-2000, FAX (734) 485-0704
Web site: *www.highscope.org,* E-mail: *press@highscope.org*

Editor: Lynn Taylor
Text design, illustrations, and production: Judy Seling of Seling Design
Cover design: Robin Ward

Library of Congress Cataloging-in-Publication Data
DeBruin-Parecki, Andrea.
  Letter links : alphabet learning with children's names / Andrea
DeBruin-Parecki and Mary Hohmann.
      p. cm.
    Includes bibliographical references.
      ISBN 1-57379-143-1 (soft cover : alk. paper)
    1. English language--Alphabet--Study and teaching (Early childhood)
    2. Names--Pronunciation. 3. Reading--Phonetic method. I. Hohmann,
    Mary. II. Title.
      LB1525.6.D43 2003
      372.62--dc21

                              2003011901

Printed in the United States of America
10 9 8 7 6 5 4 3

Contents

3

Letter-Linked Learning Activities 17

4

Nametags and Letter Links 31

Letter Links

1
Children's Name Writing and Recognition—An Early Literacy Milestone

Names are complex entities that serve a variety of functions. They connect us with family and sociocultural histories; they are part of our socio-psychological identity, signifying who and what we are. Further, personal names provide a way for children to make sense of the print world as they first recognize and then learn to produce their own name.
—Janet W. Bloodgood, 1999

Welcome to *Letter Links,* in which we present a name learning system that pairs a child's printed name with a letter-linked picture of an object that starts with the same letter and sound: *Flora* and ❀, *Sam* and ✂, *Aaron* and ✈. Building on children's attachment to their own names, *Letter Links* introduces children to alphabet letter names and sounds through the letters and sounds in their names.

To help you get the most out of this book, we begin with an examination of the research on name learning and alphabetic principle on which the letter links system is based. This review provides a rationale for using letter-linked pictures with children's nametags and explains the letter-sound correspondence between children's names and letter-linked pictures. Chapter 2 offers steps for introducing letter links to the children in your classroom or child care center and their families. Chapter 3 outlines numerous strategies for using letter links to help build children's understanding of the *alphabetic principle, phonological awareness, sense of word,* and *vocabulary.* Chapter 4 provides illustrated sample sets of letter links to use with names that begin with letters and sounds common to the English language. For ease of use, the letter links are arranged alphabetically by their beginning letters and sounds.

Research on the Development of Name Writing and Name Recognition

What's in a child's name? Lots of personal investment and many opportunities for literacy learning! Indeed, a child's own name is an important personal entryway to early literacy development. The first word most children learn to recognize and write is their own name (Clay, 1975). Ferreiro and Teberosky (1982) found that the written form of a child's name is the starting point for children's own writing and their understanding of the concept of word. Learning to write their own name seems to be one important way that children begin to expand their concept of the role of alphabet letters (McGee & Richgels, 1989). As they see and write their name, children also begin to understand the difference between pictures and writing, and experience the flow of print from left to right.

As in all other areas of young children's lives, there is a developmental progression in learning to write and recognize their personal name. Hildreth (1936) demonstrated that children's ability to write their own name improved steadily from age three to six without any direct instruction in writing. They begin with aimless scribbling and move through the following stages: systematic up and down scratching, horizontal movements combined with vertical strokes, separate symbols, correctly formed letters mixed with incorrectly formed letters, and finally the correct spelling of their first name with occasional reversals or letter malformation. (See "Preschool Name Writing Samples" on pages 6 and 7.) Children begin to recognize that the written form of their name is a personal label that belongs to them. By attempting to write it, they experience an initial connection to conventional print. Their perception of their printed name also begins to change, moving from seeing it as a whole or "ideograph," to seeing it as a series of parts or individual letters.

Although children begin to recognize and write their name in some form at a very early age, this does not mean that they understand letter-sound correspondence. For example, they may not be aware that letters have a specific shape, name, or order. While they may recognize the first letter of their name, they often cannot name that letter. Rather, three-year-olds often treat all the letters in their name as one symbol that represents their name instead of viewing their name as a series of individual letters (Vallaume & Wilson, 1989). Thus, young children may first see their names as ideographs or symbolic representations of themselves in much the same way an infant sees a necklace, for example, without distinguishing the individual beads.

As children grow older, however, they begin to discriminate between drawing and writing in both form and function, realizing that a picture looks like the object it represents and the written letters name it. Early learners then start to understand that written letters stand for the spoken word that represents the actual object or action (Bloodgood, 1999). For example, they attach meaning to the written and spoken word "chair" based on their actual experience with real chairs.

Finally, children begin to understand that their names (and other written words) are formed by a particular series of letters, that these letters also have names, and that the letters correspond to the spoken sounds. These are complex concepts for young children! The English alphabet has a rather complex letter-sound code because each letter does not precisely match the sounds it represents and a letter can stand for more than one sound. Young children begin to break the letter-sound code by learning the names of the alphabet letters that have personal meaning to them. They also explore beginning sounds in words that begin with the same letter and sound ("**D**ebbie," "**d**uck," "**d**eer"), leading them to an initial understanding of both the **alphabetic principle**—the knowledge that there is a systematic relationship between letters and sounds—and **phonological awareness**—the general ability to attend to the *sounds* of language as distinct from the *meaning*. For children to understand written language, they also need to develop a **sense of word**—the ability to isolate words and hold them stable. That is, they need to understand spacing to indicate separation between one word and the next, and they need to understand that the letters **C-h-r-i-s** when written together, make up the name *Chris* every time. Names, then, offer a personally meaningful way for young children to develop the beginning skills in alphabetic principle, phonological awareness, and sense of word they need to become successful readers and writers. (Bloodgood, 1999).

When you begin to see a young child point to the first letter in her name and say, "This is me!" or you hear a young child say, *"A is for Andee!* That's my name!" you are experiencing a young child's awakening to conventional literacy skills.

Research About the Alphabetic Principle: Underlying Concepts

As we noted earlier, children's name writing is a natural bridge to acquiring the alphabetic principle. In the English language, individual alphabet letters **(graphemes)** represent speech sounds **(phonemes)** in spoken words. Thus, to read an unfamiliar word, readers scan across a word from left to right and then quickly pronounce and blend the sound associated with each letter or letter combination to produce a word. The fact that the letters in written words represent the sounds in spoken words seems self-evident to adult readers. When adults encounter one of the few words they do not automatically know how to read, they are conscious of the need to use the alphabetic principle to figure out how to say the word. Thus, most adults scan across unfamiliar words looking for groups of letters that spell familiar word parts *(trum-pet)* and blend these together to pronounce "trumpet." Young children who have not yet begun to read, however, do not understand the role that letters play in written text and are not consciously aware of the sounds in spoken language. Yet, all young children must discover the alphabetic principle in order to become fluent, independent readers (Snow, Burns, & Griffin, 1998).

Preschool Name Writing Samples

During a two-year study of name writing, psychologist Gertrude Hildreth collected and analyzed name writing samples from 85 girls and 85 boys between the ages of three and six and a half, all of whom were enrolled or applying for admission to the Lincoln School at Teachers College in New York City. The following discussion and representative signatures[1] (by years and months of age) summarize the levels of name writing development she found in her study:

Level I: Ages 3 to 3-6 Years
"Something beyond aimless scribbling appears at this level. There is considerable tendency toward the horizontal and some systematic up and down scratching."

Nancy 3-4   *Larry 3-1*

Rosalind 3-2

Level II: Ages 3-6 to 3-11 Years
"The chief improvement here is the still greater tendency toward horizontal movement with greater regularity in the vertical strokes. There is some slight tendency to make discrete symbol units, though these are scarcely recognizable as letters."

Charles 3-11

Catharine 3-6

Katharine 3-10

David 3-7

Jim 3-10

Level III: Ages 4-0 to 4-5 Years
"Separate symbol units become still more easily discerned. The waviness in imitation of adult cursive writing has almost ceased with the child's new recognition of the separate letter units. Occasionally a sample letter such as H or O is made correctly, but for the most part the letter units are not recognizable as such. There is more constriction in space."

Elizabeth 4-0   *Harriet 4-4*

Judith 4-4   *Edna 4-3*

Sam 4-5   *Mary 4-4*

[1]*Reprinted with permission of the Society for Research in Child Development.*

Level IV: Ages 4-6 to 4-11 Years

"At this level we find correctly formed letters mixed with many incorrectly formed. There is little correct spelling of an entire name; letters are often omitted or rearranged. The letters written do not match the name very closely. This age range is definitely for those children a transition point in writing."

(handwriting)	*John 4-6*	ARPIOPIAL+	*Mary 4-9*	UAN	*Joan 4-11*
BBBBBC	*Bobbie 4-11*	qⱳA		*Juan 4-6*	TDY	*Judy 4-9*
MB	*Marcia B. 4-11*	VIR⌐	*Virginia 4-7*		

Level V: Ages 5-0 to 5-6 Years

"Here we find correct spelling of a first name or nickname, but there are occasional reversals or letter malformations. There is more firmness in control, more regularity, more ease and rapidity of writing, and better alignment. The children find pleasure and fun in writing."

TOHN	*John 5-6*	ANN E	*Anne 5-2*
HELEN	*Helen 5-0*	DAVID	*David 5-3*
BOBBIE	*Bobbie 5-2*	RUTH	*Ruth 5-3*

Level VI: Ages 5-6 to 5-11 Years

"Improvement in every respect is obvious. There are still occasional letter reversals. The writing from child to child is more similar in style and more regular than formerly."

JIMMY	*Jimmy 5-8*	PETER	*Peter 5-7*	JACK	*Jack 5-9*
IRIS	*Iris 5-9*	ELINOR	*Elinor 5-8*	HELEN	*Helen 5-7*
JOAN	*Joan 5-8*	YOUNG	*Young 5-8*		

Level VII: Ages 6-0 to 6-5 Years

"The chief improvement at this stage is in speed of writing. The consistency of results is surprising considering the small number of cases. Many of these children can also write their last name."

BIII	*Bill 6-3*	DONALD	*Donald 6-0*
Brooks	*Brooks 6-4*	LENORE	*Lenore 6-0*
SALLY	*Sally 6-4*	HENRY	*Henry 6-5*

Children need to understand three main concepts to discover and use the alphabetic principle. First, at the most basic level, children must **learn that printed text conveys a meaning.** Understanding that a McDonald's sign consisting of integrated print and golden arches says "McDonald's" and means *a place to get food* is critical to becoming a reader. At this early phase of literacy development, children's ideas about how written text works and how the printed word and symbolic representation are related are not connected to their knowledge of alphabet letters or to the sounds in language. Instead, they are related to their emerging awareness and understanding of symbols and representation. For most preschoolers, the word *McDonald's,* coupled with the golden arches, symbolizes the meaning of the restaurant.

A second concept that children must gain is the ability to **attend to the sound features of a word** rather than to its meaning. Phonological awareness allows children consciously to attend to the sound chunks within words such as syllables, rhyming words, and words with similar sounds at their beginnings or endings. Phonemic awareness occurs when children can hear, separate, and manipulate single sounds (phonemes) within words. Phonological and phonemic awareness do not require knowledge of alphabet letters because children's attention is on the sounds in spoken words without reference to written words. Children do not have to have fully developed phonemic awareness in order to grasp the alphabetic principle. However, they must have developed some rudimentary abilities to hear word onset (the sound before the vowel) and rime (the sound after the onset) such as /m/ /om/, /k/ /ar/, and /sh/ /ip/ (Stahl & Murray, 1994). More fully developed phonemic awareness, for example, being able to say each sound in the word cat, /k/ /a/ /t/, develops after children begin to read.

The third foundational concept that children must have before discovering the alphabetic principle is the ability to **recognize alphabet letters fairly fluently.** They must be able to distinguish an *M* from a *D*, for example, in order to later attach a unique sound to each letter. To use the alphabetic principle effectively, children need to recognize alphabet letters quickly so that their attention is free to work on remembering the sound associated with that letter (Adams, 1990).

Gaining Letter Knowledge Through Meaningful Interaction

Even with these three foundational concepts firmly in place, many children still do not discover the alphabetic principle without support from a parent or teacher. Children who can recognize rhyming words, detect that two words have the same beginning sound, and identify all the alphabet letters by name still may not necessarily recognize that the alphabet letters in words align with sounds in words (Byrne & Fielding-Barnsley, 1991). Learning the sounds (phonemes) associated with a few letters, however, does seem to lead most children to discover the alphabetic principle. Teachers can guide this process by helping children invent their own spellings and drawing children's attention to letter-sound associations as they write and read together.

"Systematic teaching of the alphabet, one letter per week, is not as successful as teaching children letters that are meaningful to them" (Morrow, 1988, p. 131). Since children learn the alphabetic principle best when it relates to them personally, they need to work and play in environments rich with print and text, supported by knowledgeable teachers who engage them in reading and writing experiences closely related to their own lives, interests, and abilities. Clearly, learning to write and name letters is an interactive process involving both children and supportive adults.

Why Use Letter Links?

Young children learn alphabet letter names and sounds by talking about and attempting to write their own name and other printed words they encounter on a regular basis such as *Stop, Art Area,* and *I love you.* Pretty soon, they can identify themselves by the first letter of their own name, and soon after they can identify others the same way. They are able to differentiate between themselves and others using the written letter, for example, *A* stands for *Andee, D* stands for *David,* and *F* stands for *Flora.*

Children seem to move in a natural learning progression from name writing into letter knowledge. They begin by being unable to name a single letter and progress to learning that letters are unique and each has its own sound or sounds. While children use a variety of strategies to come to this conclusion, it is clear that learning to identify, read, and write their own name has a major influence on this progression. When such an obvious and accessible learning tool is readily available to teachers, it is imperative that they make use of it. *Letter Links* provides a means for doing so. We provide a child's nametag in two pieces: The first piece displays the **child's name** with the first letter highlighted—*Flora;* the second piece displays a letter-linked **picture** of an object that begins with the same letter and sound as the child's name, in Flora's case, a flower— ❀. (See sample at right.) Children need to understand that letters have both names and sounds. The **letter links learning system** assists with this task by connecting the alphabetic principle with phonological awareness, two important skills young children need to develop as early literacy learners.

Most early childhood teachers provide their children with nametags or with symbols in distinctive shapes that bear the child's name—for example, *Dan* printed on the shape of a truck, *Shantel* printed on the shape of bell, and so forth. So, why should they change from using nametags or symbols to using letter links? Nametags alone enable adults to identify children's work and belongings and help children learn to recognize their printed name. With daily exposure, most young children will learn to recognize their own name. It will take them much longer, however, to learn to recognize the names of all their classmates and to use nametags to locate the work and belongings of others. Symbols with names written on them enable both adults and children to identify children's work and belongings quickly and easily. Even the youngest child soon learns that her symbol is the moon, Dan's is the truck, Shantel's is the bell, and so on. Children can also learn to write their own name from looking at and attempting to copy the name written on their symbol. Symbols also help children negotiate the classroom with ease because children can tell at a glance whose things belong to whom. Because the distinctively shaped symbols are so easy to read, however, they may in some cases overshadow the printed version of the name they bear.

Letter links, on the other hand, come in two distinct parts—the nametag and the letter-linked image. Separate but used together, these two pieces combine the distinctive print features of nametags with the easy identity of symbols and have the added literacy value of linking the two through common initial letters and sounds. Further, letter links support the child's developmental progression from symbols to print and from ideographs to letters and names. The letter links learning system provides two ways for a young child to recognize her own name and the names of classmates: ***a written nametag,*** which will gradually take on greater significance as she learns to distinguish its parts and write her own name conventionally; and her ***letter-linked picture,*** which she and other children can easily recognize and which will gradually fall into disuse because she will no longer need it. Initially, a young child appears to see her written name, *Flora,* as environmental print that stands for her in much the same way she sees the letters and pictures on the Cheerios box as standing for *Cheerios,* Nike and the Nike swoosh standing for *Nike,* the yellow and green John Deere logo standing for *John Deere,* and so forth. When we provide her with a written nametag— *Flora*— and a drawing of a flower—❀—she basically has two symbols or ideographs that stand for her. Over time, as she begins to distinguish the letters in her name, she will become more attached to *Flora* and less reliant on ❀, which will eventually become obsolete as she learns to read her own and her classmate's names. In the meantime, every child can read every other child's letter-linked picture before they have any understanding of printed names and letters.

The way the young child begins to write her name may be the best window we currently have on how she understands and begins to decode her written nametag. Her first "signatures" are scrawls and scribbles, generally one continuous form with no distinct parts or letters, indicating, for example, that she sees her written nametag as one continuous whole. Next, she begins to write her name as a series of patterns that include repeated elements such as lines, balls, squiggles, and even letter-like forms indicating that now she sees her written name as a series of parts or elements. After this stage, she begins to distinguish and reproduce actual letters in her name, beginning with the first letter and generally followed by the last letter, and these letters appear in her signature. Finally, she is able to write her entire first name, *Flora,* using conventional letters (though some may be reversed or upside down), indicating that now she sees her name as a particular sequence of distinct parts or letters. She may or may not know the names of the letters and likely does not associate the letters with the sounds they make in her name. This sound-letter connection will come later with more writing and reading experience.

Since the letter-linked picture also starts with and includes the first letter of her name, it may actually help the child to begin to see the initial letter in her written name. Moreover, since her name and her letter link also begin with the same sound, she may also connect the first sound in her name to the first letter or letter combination in her name.

Understanding the Letter-Sound Correspondences in Letter Links

The idea behind the letter links learning system is to have each child in your class select a picture that starts with the same letter and sound as the child's name. Therefore, the letter links in this book are organized alphabetically by their beginning letters and sounds.

A look at the contents or a flip through the book quickly reveals that there are more than 26 types of letter links. Why are there more sets of letter links than there are letters in the alphabet? Because many letters represent more than one sound. Let's start with the vowels *A, E, I, O,* and *U.* Each vowel can be pronounced as a short vowel as at the beginning of *Andy, Evan, Iggy, Oscar,* and *Umberto;* or as a long vowel as at the beginning of *Ada, Eva, Irene, Okalani,* and *Ukiah.* Further, some initial vowels change their sound when they are followed by the letter *r* as in *Arthur, Ernest, Orrin,* and *Ursula.* Finally, some initial vowels, when followed by a second vowel, change sound yet again as in *Audrey, Eileen,* and *Eugene.* So, for example, depending on the influence of other letters immediately following it, the letter *E* can represent five different sounds at the beginning of five different names. Listen to the way the sound of the initial *E* changes as you say *Evan, Eva, Eileen, Ernest,* and *Eugene!*

When we listen to initial consonants, we find that two letters, *C* and *G,* have both hard and soft sounds as in *Caitlin* and *Cindy, Gabby* and *Georgia.* Then there are the digraphs *Ch, Ph, Sh, Th,* and *Wh* that represent a different set of sounds as in *Chelsea, Philip, Shemeka, Theo,* and *Whitney* as well as the *ch* that sounds like /sh/ as in *Cher.* The blends—*Bl, Br, Chr, Cl, Cr, Dr, Fl, Fr, Kr, Pl, Pr, Sc, Sk, Sl, Sn, Sp, St, Sw,* and *Tr*—are not new sounds. For example, the *F* at the beginning of *Fergus, Flora,* and *Frieda,* always sounds like /f/, but the *F* and the *l* at the beginning of *Flora* are blended so closely together in speech, that it made sense to us to provide letter-linked pictures that begin with blends for children whose names begin with blends. Hence, *Flora* and ✿.

Between long and short vowels, vowels influenced by *r* and by other vowels *(au, ei, eu),* hard and soft consonants, digraphs, and blends, we offer 67 initial sounds in children's names represented by 26 letters and letter combinations! Now you can see why the alphabetic code is difficult for young children to decipher!

While we have tried to provide letter-linked pictures that match the beginning letters and sounds of most children's names, some children in your class may have names that begin with sounds that do not correspond to the sound the initial letter represents in English. For example, in Spanish, the letter *J* is close in sound to /h/, so to English speakers, the name *José* sounds as if it were written *Hosé.* In this situation, when the first letter in a child's name does not correspond with the sound of this book's letter links that start with that letter, you have two choices:

(1) You can use the child's photograph as his letter-linked image (printing the first letter of his name in each corner).

(2) With the aid of the child's family, you can draw an object that in his language starts with the same letter and sound as his name. For José's letter link, therefore, you might draw a jirafa (giraffe) or a jarra (pitcher), including a *J* in each corner of his letter link. When José's letter link is a jirafa and Josh's letter link is juggler, the children in your class will discover that *J* represents the sound /h/ in Spanish and the sound /j/ in English.

References

Adams, M. (1990). *Beginning to read: Thinking and learning about print.* Cambridge, MA: MIT Press.

Bloodgood, J. W. (1999). What's in a name? Children's name writing and literacy acquisition. *Reading Research Quarterly, 34*(3), 342–367.

Byrne, B. (1996). The learnability of the alphabetic principle: Children's initial hypotheses about how print represents spoken language. *Applied Linguistics, 17,* 401–426.

Bryne, B., & Fielding-Barnsley, R. (1991). Evaluation of a program to teach phonemic awareness to young children. *Journal of Educational Psychology, 83,* 451–455.

Clay, M. (1975). *What did I write?* Auckland, NZ: Heinemann Educational Books.

Ferreiro, E., & Teberosky, A. (1982). *Literacy before schooling.* Portsmouth, NH: Heinemann.

Hildreth, G. (1936). Developmental sequences in name writing. *Child Development, 7,* 291–303.

McGee, L. M., & Richgels, D. J. (1989). "K is Kristen's": Learning the alphabet from a child's perspective. *The Reading Teacher, 43*(3), 216–225.

Morrow, L. M. (1988). *Literacy development in the early years: Helping children read and write.* Upper Saddle River, NJ: Prentice-Hall.

Snow, C., Burns., S., & Griffin, P. (1998). *Preventing reading difficulties in young children.* Washington, DC: National Academy Press.

Stahl, S., & Murray, B. (1994). Defining phonological awareness and its relationship to early reading. *Journal of Educational Psychology, 86,* pp. 221–234.

Vallaume, S., & Wilson, L. (1989). Preschool children's explorations of letters in their own names. *Applied Psycholinguistics 10,* 283–300.

2
Getting Started With Letter Links

Now that you are familiar with the research behind letter links, the reasons for using them, and the letter-sound correspondences they entail, you are ready to begin using them! Here are the steps we suggest for introducing them to the children in your classroom or center.

Step 1: Learn Names

Learn the preferred name of each child in your class. For example, you may read the name *DeLawan Jamal Jordan* on a child's enrollment form and assume that this particular child is called DeLawan. His family, however, may call him DeLawan, Dela, Lawan, Wan, Jamal, Mal, DJ, Boomer, or Leon. If you prepare a nametag for him that says *DeLawan* and he refers to himself as Lawan, the whole notion of starting letter learning with the child's personal name is already lost. Asking a child who considers his name to be Lawan to choose a letter link that starts with *D* for *DeLawan* is totally confusing to the child. We know, because we've made this mistake ourselves!

Step 2: Learn Pronunciations

Learn how to pronounce each child's name in the way the child is used to hearing it spoken. Find out from family members how they pronounce the child's name and pronounce it that way yourself. *Cheri,* for example, might be pronounced to sound like *Sherry* or *Cherry.* You may pronounce *Eva* with a long *E,* while the child in your class and her family may pronounce it with a short *E* as in *Evan.* It is important not to change a child's name to suit the way you may be used to hearing it. If you see a child's written name and don't know how to pronounce it, ask a family member to say it for you. If you have trouble hearing or remembering how it is pronounced, write it out phonetically for yourself and practice saying it until you can pronounce it fluently.

Step 3: Make Multiple Nametags

Make several nametags for each teacher and child using the names children go by (that is, the names you gathered in step one). Print each child's name clearly. Capitalize the first letter and make it darker than the rest. If you need a guide, look at the sample nametags that appear in Chapter 4 in this book. (All the names and pictures may be duplicated.) If you decide to print nametags on the computer, choose a font or style of print similar to the one used in Chapter 4, that is, one that uses a **sans serif typeface,** such as *Century Gothic.* Print the first letter of the name in **boldface type.** You may wish to print some nametags on self-sticking labels.

Step 4: Child Selects a Letter-Linked Picture

Have each child select a picture that starts with the same letter and sound as the first letter (or letter combination) in the child's name. To do this, find a time to sit for a few minutes with each child during the enrollment process, on a home visit, at arrival time, or during snack time. As you sit with Flora, for example, turn to the *Fl* page and ask her which picture she would like to choose to go with her nametag. She may select the flag, flamingo, flower, or flute. If another child in her class has already selected one of these images, tell her so. You may then wish to cover it up, replace it with your own drawing of one of the other choices at the bottom of the page, or simply read the additional choices to her. Once Flora has chosen her letter-linked image, pencil her name lightly next to it to help you keep track of the pictures children select.

Step 5: Teachers Select Letter Links

Repeat step 4 with the teachers and other adults (including parents) who regularly interact with the children in your classroom. Have each adult select an image that starts with the same letter and sound as the initial letter in the adult's first name. You or another adult in your classroom may have asked children to address you by title: Miss Sue, Mrs. Jones, Mr. Dan. In such cases, it is important to include only one word on your nametag so children can easily understand the letter link between the name on your nametag and your picture. Miss Sue, for example, may print *Sue* on her nametag and a select an *S* link (saw, scissors, seal, sun), or she may print *Miss* on her nametag and select an *M* link (maraca, mitten, moon, motorcycle). Alternatively, she may print *Miss* on one nametag followed by an *M* picture, and print *Sue* on a second nametag followed by an *S* picture: "I have two nametags and pictures because I have two words in my name," she might say to children. "'Miss' and 'Sue'."

Step 6: Make Multiple Letter Links for Each Child

Either make your own letter-linked pictures or use this book to photocopy multiple copies of each child's letter link and then cut them out. To ensure durability, you may wish to

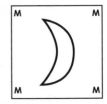

copy them on labels or on heavy paper or card stock, laminate them, or cover them with clear contact paper. You may wish to do this step with parents on a home visit or at a parent meeting to acquaint families with the letter-linked pictures and nametags so they can use them at home in the activities described in Chapter 3.

Step 7: Identify Each Child's Belongings With Nametags and Letter-Linked Pictures

Hang children's nametags and letter links around the room to designate things and places that belong to the child: a coat hook, cubby, personal storage tub, toothbrush (small version on adhesive tape); on the snack jobs chart, the jobs chart, and so on. Keep the nametags and letter links posted throughout the year so children will always know where to find their written name, and so that even young children and those new to the program can find their own and other's belongings by using the letter links learning system.

Step 8: Write the Child's Name and Draw the Letter-Linked Image on the Child's Work

Write the child's name and draw the appropriate letter link on the child's work as needed. Share this task with the child. When you draw a child's letter link, use the pictures in this book as a guide. Include telling details and do not worry when you simplify or modify the image based on your own drawing ability. A child named Cathy, for example, will recognize her "cat" drawing and yours just as she recognizes her own signature and your print version of her name.

3
Letter-Linked Learning Activities

Once each child has selected a letter-linked image that starts with the same letter and sound as the child's name, you can begin to use the nametags and letter links as teaching and learning tools! The following 25 learning activities will help you support and extend children's emerging understanding of the alphabetic principle, phonological awareness, sense of word, and vocabulary. The activities are numbered for easy reference and are meant to be used, revisited, and adapted to your particular children as needed over the course of a year. The activities can also be supplemented by the letter recognition, letter-sound, and phonological awareness activities described in *Fee, Fie, Phonemic Awareness—130 Prereading Activities for Preschoolers* by Mary Hohmann.[1]

Activities Related to the Alphabetic Principle

Activities 1–16 actively engage children in recognizing their printed name, writing their name, identifying the letters in their name, and associating letter sounds with the letters in their name. By drawing their attention in a meaningful way to the letters and sounds in their own name, these activities will help children establish a firm foundation for deciphering the alphabetic code. Note that activities 2, 5–7, and 1–12 can be used by parents and family members at home either as is or with some modification.

Name recognition

1. **Identify names and letter links.** Make a set of nametags and letter links in two or three sizes for each child and adult in your class. At a **transition time,** spread all the nametags and letter links face up on a table or the floor

---

[1]To order this High/Scope Press publication, go to *www.highscope.org/welcome.asp.*

where children can easily see and reach them. Ask the children to choose their own name and letter link and take them to their small-group meeting place (or whatever event comes next in the daily routine).

At a **transition time,** provide a set of nametags and letter links in a box, bag, or spread out on a tray. Hold up a child's nametag and letter link and say "It's this person's turn to hop to the table for snack [or whatever is next]." Wait for one of the children to recognize and say the name of the child whose nametag and letter link you are holding.

At **large-group times,** use nametags and letter links from time to time to designate turns—to choose the next song to sing, to decide which game to play next, to add on to the story you are telling, and so forth. For example, hold up a child's nametag and letter link and say "It's this person's turn to decide the place in the room we should march to next."

2. **Include names and letter-linked pictures on the message board.** Each day on the **message board** write a message that refers to one or more children by their name and letter link. Give children a chance to read the names and messages. Here, for example, are messages like the ones you might write:

"Flora ❀ ⇨ grandma's ⌂." *(Flora's at her grandma's house today.)*

"Stella ☆'s birthday 🎂 " *(It's Stella's birthday.)*

"Aaron ✈ and Seth ✂ Big box ❑ ⇨ house ⌂"
(Aaron and Seth: There's a big box to use for your house.)

3. **Match nametags.** Make a set of nametag cards that will allow children to play a nametag memory transition game. Make sure that all the nametag cards are the same size. Include in the set two nametags for each child. Cover the nametag cards with clear contact paper for durability. At the end of **small-group, planning, recall, or morning greeting time,** spread all the nametag cards face down on the floor. Have each children take turns turning over a card, identifying the name, and leaving the card face up. When two cards turn up with the same name, have the named child hop (jump, skip, or crawl) to the next activity. Let the children know where the nametag cards will be stored (for example, in the toy area) in case they want to play with them during work or choice time.

4. **Identify names.** At a **transition time,** place a set of nametags only (without the letter-linked pictures) in a basket or bag. Draw and hold up a child's nametag and say "It's this person's turn to jump to the planning table [or whatever event is next in your daily routine]." Wait for one of the children to recognize and say the name of the child whose nametag you are displaying. If no one can identify the name, hold up the letter-linked image that goes with it.

At **large-group times,** use nametags from time to time to designate which child will choose the next song to sing, decide which game to play next, add on to the story you are telling, and so forth. For example, hold up a child's nametag and say "It's this person's turn to decide which music we should put on for dancing." If no one can identify the name, hold up the letter-linked image that goes with the name.

At a **transition time,** once most children can identify their name without referring to their letter-linked pictures, put two sets of nametags in a basket or bag. To begin the activity, say something like this: "I have two nametags for each person in my basket. When I hold up your name, come and get it. When you have your two nametags, one for each hand, you can go wash your hands."

Name writing

5. **Sign in.** In some preschool centers, children see their parents or guardians **sign in** when they drop them off at the center and sign out when they leave at the end of the session. For these children, signing in themselves will make particular sense. For others, signing in can become a daily part of the class routine that allows them to write their name and examine the way others write. On a large whiteboard, blackboard, or sheet of butcher or chart paper, place the children's nametags and letter-linked pictures in alphabetical order:

Leave plenty of room for children to write and adequate space between names. Even though you have provided each child with a sample of his or her name to look at, remember that children learn to see and write their name in stages. You will see these stages in all their variety as children sign in each day. If you are using paper, date and save each piece for a daily record of how each child is seeing and writing his or her name. If you are using a whiteboard or a black-board, use paper once a month to date and save. If all children do not have a chance to sign in as they arrive or during morning gathering, assure them that they can sign in during work or choice time, before lunch, or at some other time that day.

Comment from time to time on what you see children writing as they sign in: "You made a *J* just like the *J* in James." "Mira and Madison, both your names start with the letter *M!*"

6. **Sign up for a job.** Rather than attaching children's nametags and letter links to **daily job charts,** invite children to sign up for these jobs by writing their name or their name and letter link next to the job they have chosen. Here they will not have an immediate model to follow as on the daily sign-in sheet. You will find that some children go right ahead and sign their name in the manner that makes sense to them. Other children will prefer to find their nametag and use it to remind them about the letters they want to write. Here, for example, is a sample chart:

Again, whether you construct the chart on paper or a reusable board, allow plenty of room for children to write their names. Comment on the way children are writing their names. For example, you might say, "Zarius, you wrote your name using lines and dots. It looks like the way you write your name on the sign-in sheet!" "Madison, I see you made an *M* at the beginning of your name, just like the *M* on your nametag." "Anna, I see the *A* at the beginning of your name and another *A* toward the end!" "Zach, there's the *Z* at the beginning of your name. And you and Anna both have *A*'s in your names."

7. **Make a name book.** Find an empty three-ring binder and a set of tabbed pages. Print each child's name on a tab and divide the binder into as many sections as there are children in your small group. At **small-group time,** give each child a three-hole-drilled piece of paper and ask the children to make a page about their name for the name book. Anticipate that children will respond with a variety of ideas, ways of writing their name (from scribbling to letters), and even drawings. As children complete the pages, date each page (by hand or have the children do it with a date stamp). Talk with each of the children about what the page says about their name, how they have written their name, and the letters they have used. Have each child put the page in the binder. You may also want each child to write or draw on the cover, spine, and back of this book, especially if the binder is the type with front, back, and spine pockets. Repeat this small-group time periodically so you and the children can see how their name writing progresses as they begin to understand more about names and writing. Whenever you do this activity, no matter what a child's stage of name writing is at the time, children will learn more from watching and listening to one another write and talk about writing.

8. **Make nametag flaps.** In this **small-group-time activity,** children write their name on nametags so they can add their name to the *Letter Links* book itself. Beforehand, make blank nametags the size of the nametags in *Letter Links.* At small-group time, give each child in your group several blank nametags. Ask the children to write their name on the blank nametags. As children work, move from child to child. Ask each child to select one of their nametags and help them tape (mystic tape works best) the top of their nametag (as a flap) to the top of the nametag on the page that bears their letter link. At the end of this small group, for example, you might have several nametag flaps attached to some pages and a single nametag flap attached to others. With the children, look at the pages to which they have taped their names. Finally, ask the children for ideas about what they can do with their extra nametags. During the year, as children become more adept at writing their name, they may wish to replace these nametags with new ones they write.

Letter recognition

9. **Compare names and letter-linked pictures.** Prepare a basket of capital letters that includes all the initial letters of the names of the children in your class. At a **small-group transition time,**[1] give each of the children their nametag and letter-linked image. Ask the children to find another person with the same first letter in their name and letter on their letter link (for example, Flora and Fatima). When pairs of children find each other, have them tell you the name of their common letter and then have them go to the

---

[1]To start off, try these transitions at the end of a small-group activity (small group, snack, planning, recall). Later on, you may wish to try the activities during transitions that involve more children.

snack table (or whatever happens next in your program). If they cannot find a person whose name starts with the same letter as theirs, have them find a plastic alphabet letter that is the same as the first letter in their name and on their letter link.

At another **small-group transition time,** give each of the children their nametag and letter-linked picture, and ask them to find another child who has a letter different from theirs at the beginning of their name and on their letter-linked picture (for example, **W**ill and **M**ax). When pairs of children find each other, have them tell you the names of the two different letters they have found.

When most children are beginning to write their names using letters, here is another variation of this **transition activity** to try. Give each of the children their nametag and letter-linked image, and ask them to find another child who has a letter in his or her name that is the same as any letter in their name. For example, Emma and Max might show you that they both have the letter *M* and the letter *a* in their names, while Josh and Colin might notice that their names both have the letter *o*.

10. **Match initial letters.** Use the set of nametag cards (two nametags for each child) described in activity 3. At the end of **morning greeting time,** spread all the nametag cards face down on the floor. Have each of the children take turns turning over a card, identifying the first letter in the name on the card, and leaving the card face up for the rest of the game. When two cards turn up that start with the same letter, have the child who notices and names the letter hop (jump, skip, or crawl) to the planning table. Let the children know where the nametag cards will be stored in case they want to play with them during work or choice time.

You can also make a set of memory cards using two copies each of each child's letter-linked picture. At the end of a **small-group transition,** turn all the letter links face down on the floor. Have children take turns turning over a card and identifying the letter on the image. When two cards turn up that bear the same letter, have the child who notices and names the letter hop (jump, skip, crawl) to whatever comes next in the daily routine.

11. **Find name letters in alphabet books.** After reading an alphabet book with a child at **work or choice time, morning greeting,** or before **rest time,** ask each of the children to look at their nametag and then to find a word in the book that starts with the same letter as their name. For example, you might say, "Flora, where's the page with the letter *F* like the *F* in *Flora?*" If she is able to find the *F* page with relative ease, you might say, "Flora, what's another letter in your name?" (Flora says, *"A."*) "Where's the *A* page?"

12. **Look for name letters on a walk.** On a **walk around the neighborhood** (or wherever you walk with children), have children hold or wear their nametags and letter-linked pictures so they can see the letters right side up.

As they walk, ask them to look around for the letters in their name. Some children will focus on finding the first letters in their name; others will see some of the other letters in their name. Talk with children about the letters they find:

Ahmed: "Look, there's my *A!* And another. Two *A*'s!"

You: "Ahmed, you found the *A* at the beginning of *Airport* and the *A* at the beginning of *Avenue.*"

Photograph or write down the letters children find and the words they find them in. Here is an example of the kind of notes (or photos) you might take:

Ahmed: Airport Ave

Douglas: Dom's Donuts

Flora: For Sale

Sharonda: For Sale

During a **small-group time** following this walk, you might ask the children to write (or copy from your notes) the words they saw on their walk and add these word pages to their sections of the name book started in activity 7. If you took photos, they may wish to tape the photos of the signs to their pages as well.

Letter-sound correspondence

13. **Identify initial letter sounds in names.** At a **transition time,** hold up a child's nametag, say the child's name, make the sound represented by the first letter, and ask the child what letter in his or her name makes that sound. For example, you might have an exchange like the one that follows:

You: "Here's Darren's name. It starts with the sound /d/. Darren, what letter makes the /d/ sound at the beginning of your name?"

Darren: "Darren, *D. D* makes the /d/ sound."

You: "Okay, the *D* makes the /d/ sound at the beginning of *Darren!* You can get your coat, Darren."

If the child whose name you are holding does not yet make the letter-sound connection, usually another child who is beginning to understand this relationship will help out:

You: "Lydia, your name starts with the /l/ sound. What letter makes that /l/ sound?"

Lydia: *"Lydia!* /l/, /l/."

You:	"Yes, *Lydia* starts with the /l/ sound. Who can tell what letter in Lydia's name makes the /l/ sound?"
Max:	"I know. *L* makes the /l/ sound."
You:	"The *L* at the beginning of *Lydia* makes the /l/ sound. Lydia, you can get your coat."

To vary this **transition activity,** name the initial letter in a child's name and ask for the sound that letter makes, as in this example:

You:	"Here's Tristan's name. Tristan, your name starts with a *T.* What sound does the *T* make at the beginning of your name?"
Tristan:	*"Tristan, /t/, the /t/ sound."*
You:	"The *T* at the beginning of *Tristan* makes the /t/ sound."

14. **Identify initial letter sounds in letter links.** At **transition time,** spread a set of the children's and teachers' letter links face down on the floor. Have each child, in turn, turn a letter link face up, say what it is, and identify the letter (printed in each corner) and the sound it starts with. The game might start like this:

You:	"I'm going to start." (You turn over a letter link.) "It's a train! I can see by looking in the corner that the word *train* starts with the letter *T.* And the *T* at the beginning of *train* makes a /t/ sound. (Pause) Okay, let's go around the circle. Brian, it's your turn to turn over a letter link."
Brian:	(Turns over a cat.) "I got a cat!"
You:	"You turned over the cat. What can you tell us about letter or sound the word *cat* starts with?"
Brian:	"Cat. Here's the *C!* It has a kind of a /k/ sound. Cat!"
You:	"Cat does start with the letter *C.* It makes the /k/ sound at the beginning of the word *cat.* (Pause) Okay, off you go to wash your hands, Brian. Arles, it's your turn to turn over a letter link... ."

15. **Play I-spy-a-letter-and-a-sound in a nametag.** At a **small-group transition time,** spread a set of children's and teachers' nametags, including your own, face up on the floor. Include a few extra nametags in the set so the last child still has several letters and sounds to choose from. Have each child, in turn, spy a letter at the beginning of a name and say the sound it makes. The game might start like this:

You:	"I spy a letter at the beginning someone's name that's a *P* and sounds like /p/! I spy the name (pause to give children a chance to hunt for a name beginning with *P*. If no one spies it, find it yourself.) I spy *Peter*. (Take the nametag.) Who wants to spy the letter and sound at the beginning of another name? Rhoda!"
Rhoda:	"I spy *R*. It's /r/, *Rhoda!*"
You:	"Rhoda, you spied the letter *R* that makes the /r/ sound at the beginning of *Rhoda!*" (Rhoda takes the her nametag.)

16. **Play I-spy-a-letter-and-a-sound in a letter-linked picture.** At a **small-group transition time,** play the game described in activity 15, this time using a set of the children's and teachers' letter links rather than their nametags. Include a few extra letter-linked pictures in the set so the last child still has several letters and sounds to choose from. Have each child, in turn, spy a letter in the corner of a logo and say the sound it makes. The game might start like this:

You:	"I spy something that starts with the /h/ sound and the letter *H.*" (Pause for the children to locate such a letter link.)
Children:	"House! Hat!"
You:	*"House* and *hat* both start with the /h/ sound and the letter *H.* I was looking at the house, so I'll take the house letter link. Who's going to give us the next letter and sound to spy for? Jayla!"
Jayla:	"I spy a boat!"
You:	"You spy the boat letter link! What can you tell us about the first letter and sound in the word *boat?*"
Jayla:	"It's a *B.* Boat, boat, /b/."

Activities Related to Phonological Awareness

Activities 17–19 are designed to build on children's interest in the first sound in their name, to help them become aware of that sound, and to begin to hear it at the beginning of other spoken words. Activity 20 provides a way for children to begin to hear the sound chunks of sound, called syllables, in their names. Note that parents and family members can also do activities 18–20 at home with their preschool children.

17. **Identify alliterations.** At a **transition time,** send children to the next activity by identifying the alliterative sounds in their names and letter links. For example, you might say something like this: "Today, I'm going to say a word that starts with the same sound as your name and then say your name. When you hear two words that start with the same sound, you can go to snack. Here we go!" Say the letter link and the name slowly with an emphasis on the initial sounds: "Flower, Flora." Pause for Flora to respond. "Apple, Anna." (Pause.) "Kite, Kayla," and so forth.

At **another transition,** add a third alliterative word to each child's name and letter-linked phrase. For example, you might say, "Today, listen for three words that start with the same sound—your name and two other words that start with the same sound. Ready? Volcano, vise, Vinnie." (Pause for child to respond.) "Yes, Vinnie—*volcano, vise,* and *Vinnie* all start with the same /v/ sound! Vinnie you can get your book for nap. Listen to these words: Star, steps, Steve...," and so forth.

18. **Think of words that start with the first sound in your name.** At **snack time,** invite the children to think of and say other words (real and made up) that start with the same sound as their name. To steer children's thinking along these lines, you might say some words that start with the same sound as your name. For example, the following type of conversation might unfold:

You:	"Mary, mumps, muppets, mountain. I'm thinking of words that start with /m/ like *Mary.* Can anyone else think of some words that start with /m/?"
Children:	"Mouse." "Mike." "Moo." "Moose."
You:	*"Mouse, Mike, moo, moose, Mary!* That's a long list of words that start with /m/. Who else's name can we try?"
Theo:	"Me, Theo! Theo, thumb, thumbkin."
Children:	"Think." "Thing." "Thim."
You:	*"Thumb, thumbkin, think, thing, thim, Theo.* These are all words that start with the /th/ sound."

19. **Do and name actions that start with the first sound in your name.** At **large-group time,** as children sit on the floor, have children do actions that start with the same sound as their name:

You:	"Let's do the Peter pound! (Pause for children to pound the floor with both hands, for example.) Okay, lets try the Wanda wiggle. (Pause for chil-

dren to wiggle.) Now let's do the Stephanie stamp. (Pause for stamping). Can anyone think of an action we can do that starts with the same sound as Jameson's name?

Children: "Jump!"

You: "Let's do the Jameson jump!" (Children jump.)

As children play this game over time, they may suggest ideas on their own such as the "Felix fall," "Rhoda row," "Sara swim," "Hamed hop."

20. **Yoo-hoo children by name.** As you call to children **on the playground,** or address them in the classroom, "yoo-hoo" their name. That is, instead of singing "yoo-hoo," sing children's names on G and E, the first two pitches in the song "Rain, rain, go away." Singing children's names in this manner automatically breaks children's names into parts or large chunks of sound (syllables) and allows children to hear and become aware of the sound segments or syllables that make up their name. Sing one-syllable names using one note: "Dan" (G). Sing two-syllable names using two notes: "Flo-ra" (G-E). Sing three-syllable names using three notes: "Jam-e-son" (G-G-E); "Sha-ron-da" (E-G-E). Sing four-syllable names on four notes: "Ver-on-i-ca" (G-G-G-E or E-G-G-E) and so on. For example you might sing the following:

"Max, I'll be right there."

"Flo-ra, time to come in!"

"Ah-med, the bus is here!"

"Jam-e-son, I'm coming to play."

"Cry-stal-le-sha, it's your turn to plan."

Encourage children to sing names with you. Listen for children to begin yoo-hooing names on their own.

Activities Related to Sense of Word

These next three activities provide opportunities for children to begin to see and understand their names as discrete words.

21. **Find the word that says your name.** At a **small-group transition time,** spread a set of nametags face up on the floor. Ask children to find a word that says their name. When they find that word, they can go to the next activity.

22. **Sign cards with the word that says your name.** At **small-group time,** have the children in your group make a large card together (for example, a thank-you note, invitation, get-well card, or birthday card). When they have finished drawing, writing, and decorating the card, ask children to sign the

card by writing the word that says their name. As they write their own name, they will have the opportunity to find space that separates each word—their name—from other words/names.

23. **With three-dimensional letters, make a word that says your name.** At **small-group time,** spread out a set of nametags face up and ask the children to find the word that is their name. Then, spread a good supply of three-dimensional letters and ask the children to find the letters to make the word that is their name. Many children will use their nametag as a guide to find the letters they need. After they have spelled the word that says their name, some children may also go on to spell other words they know or can sound out. At the end of small-group time, look together at all the words the children have created.

Activities Related to Vocabulary

These activities, based on the letter links themselves, will give children the opportunity to hear, explore, and begin to use rare words, that is, words that are new to them. The more words they encounter, use, and understand as prereaders, the easier it will be for them to sound out and comprehend these words when they encounter them later on in text.

24. **Talk about the pictures in this book.** Put a copy of *Letter Links* in your book area. Look at it with children at **work, choice,** or **snack time,** for example. Talk with them about the objects pictured. Most children will be familiar with common object names such as *airplane, apple, balloon, blocks, bread, car,* and *cat.* They may be less familiar with rarer animal and object names such as *armadillo, auger, chevron, eucalyptus, flamingo, gyroscope, oryx, scallop,* and *spatula.* Accept the names children use and offer, as synonyms, the names listed at the bottom of each letter links page. For example, a conversation like this one might arise as you look together at the *Q* page:

Child:	Points to the quail. "Look a bird!"
You:	"That is a bird. It's a type of bird called a quail."
Child:	Points to the queen, quarter note, and quilt. "Here's a queen and a music thing and a blanket."
You:	"Yes, there's the queen. And this music thing is a note called a quarter note. People use it when they write music."
Child:	"Oh, a quarter note. A queen, that bird the quail, a quarter note, and a qublanket?"
You:	"Almost! A special blanket called a quilt."
Child:	"Why's it called that, a quilt?"

You: "Because it's a handmade blanket made of hundreds of pieces that are sewn or quilted together. People call it a quilt."

25. **Match real objects and animals to letter link pictures.** Bring in unfamiliar objects and animals such as cymbals and a centipede children see pictured in this book. If they are objects and animals you cannot bring to the classroom, take the children to see them at the zoo, a pet store, a construction site, marina, a dinosaur exhibit, a marching band practice, and so on. When you cannot bring in or visit objects and animals such as the Eiffel Tower, a chalet, a phoenix, or a gryphon, bring in books and photographs of them. The more opportunities children have to use and understand the words pictured in *Letter Links,* the better able they will be to comprehend them when they encounter them in print as readers.

4

Nametags and
Letter Links

A

Short A

Andrea

Letter links for names that begin with a **short A**

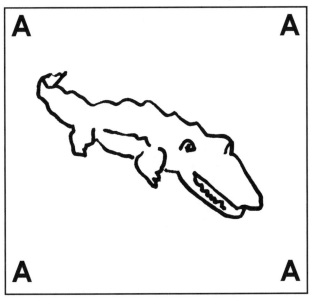

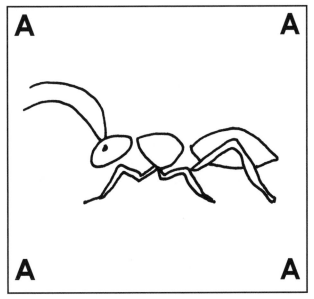

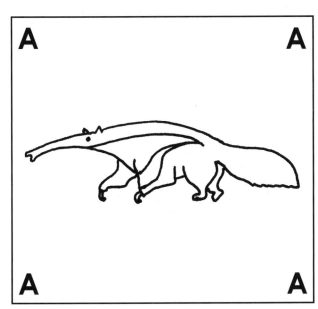

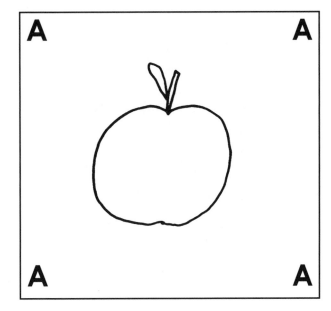

Alligator, Ant, Anteater, Apple. **Other choices:** Accordion, Ambulance.

A
Long A

Ada

Letter links for names that begin with a **long A**

A A

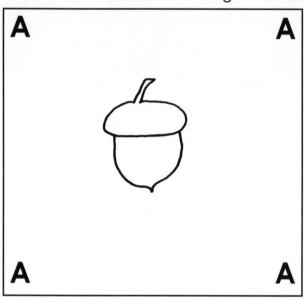

A A

A A

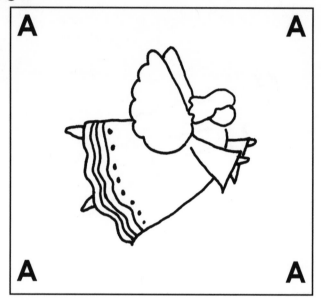

A A

A A

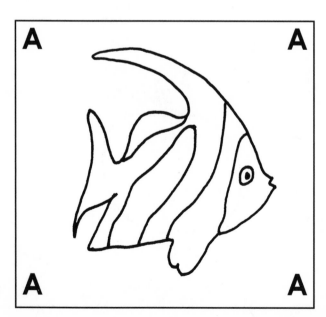

A A

A A

A A

Acorn, Angel, Angelfish, Ape. **Other choices:** Ace.

A

Ar

Aaron

Letter links for names that begin with **Ar (sounds like the /ar/ in *care*)**

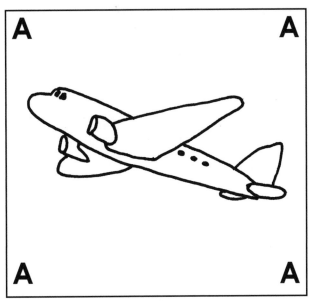

Airedale, Airplane.

A

Ar

Arthur

Letter links for names that begin with **Ar**

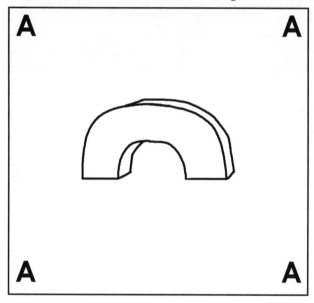

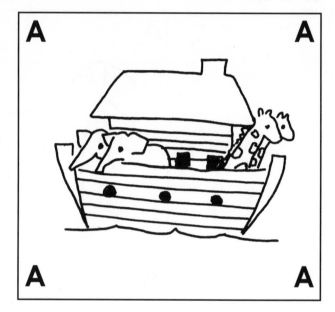

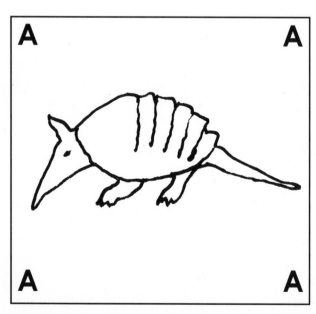

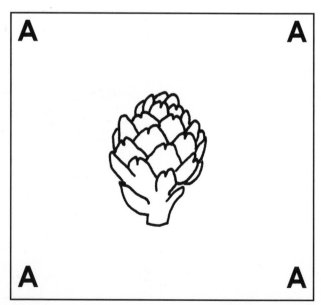

Arch, Ark, Armadillo, Artichoke. **Other choices:** Aardvark, Artist, Arm.

A **Audrey**

Au

Letter links for names that begin with **Au (sounds like /aw/)**

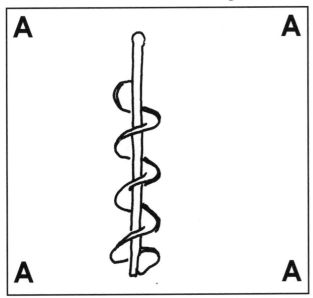

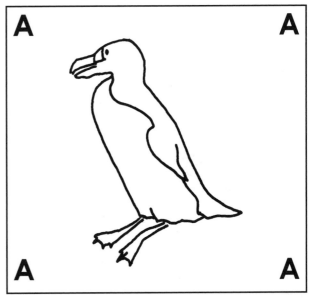

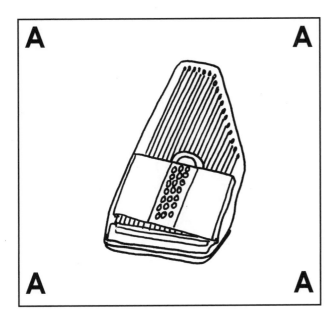

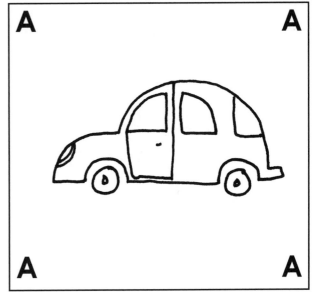

Auger, Auk, Autoharp, Automobile.

B

Benji

Letter links for names that begin with **B**

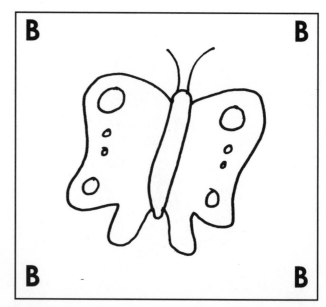

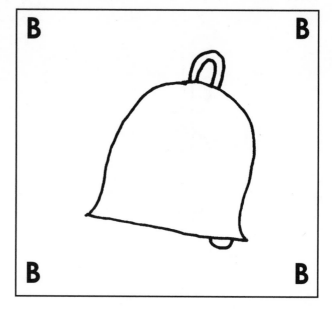

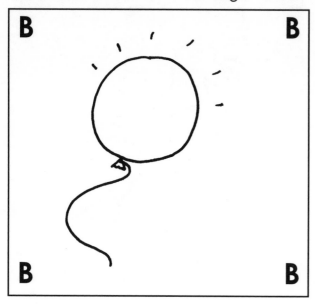

Balloon, Bell, Boat, Butterfly. **Other choices:** *Badger, Balalaika, Ball, Banana, Banjo, Bear, Beaver, Bee, Bike, Binoculars, Book, Boomerang, Buffalo.*

B

Bl

Blake

Letter links for names that begin with **Bl**

B 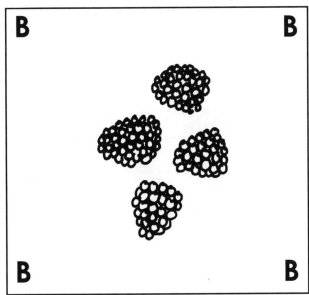 B

B B

B 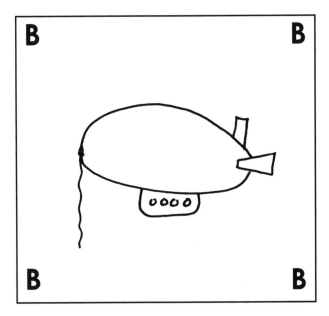 B

B B

B 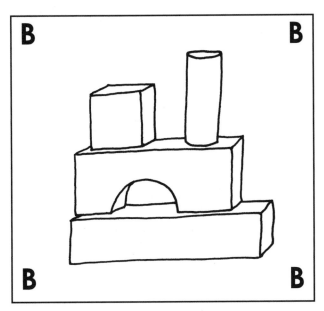 B

B B

B 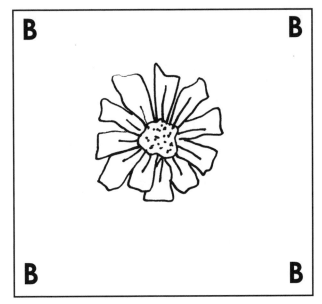 B

B B

Blackberry, Blimp, Blocks, Blossom. **Other choices:** *Blackboard, Blade, Blanket, Blueberry, Blue jeans, Blue ribbon.*

B

Br

Brianna

Letter links for names that begin with **Br**

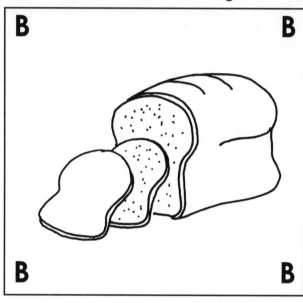

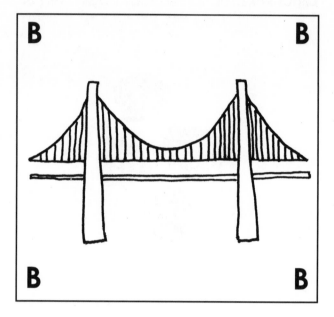

Bread, Bridge, Broccoli, Brontosaurus. **Other choices:** *Bracelet, Braid, Bride, Bridle, Briefcase, Bronco, Broom.*

Sample nametag

C

Hard C

Cathy

Letter links for names that begin with a **hard C**

Camel, Camera, Canoe, Cat. **Other choices:** *Cactus, Cake, Candle, Car, Carrot, Castanet, Castle, Caterpillar, Coat, Colander, Collar, Comb, Comet, Compass, Corn, Cow.*

Soft C

Cindy

Letter links for names that begin with a **soft C (sounds like /s/)**

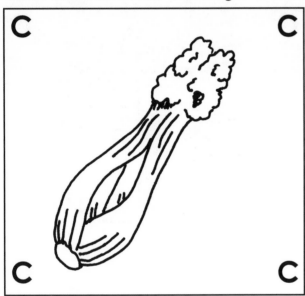

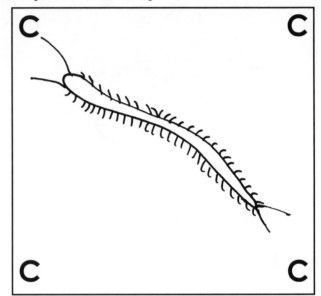

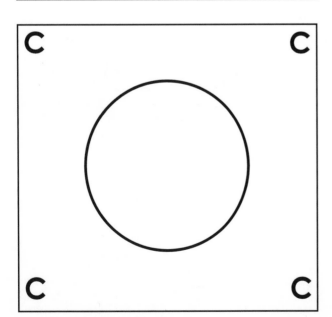

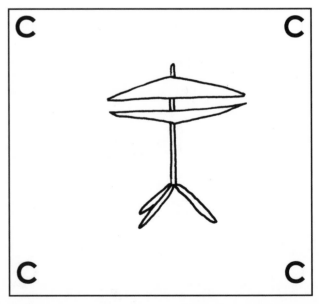

Celery, Centipede, Circle, Cymbals. **Other choices:** *Cedar, Cicada, Circus, City, Cylinder.*

Sample nametag

C

Hard Ch

C Chelsea

Letter links for names that begin with a **hard Ch**

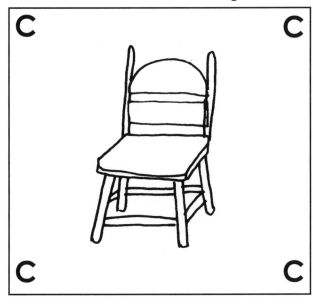

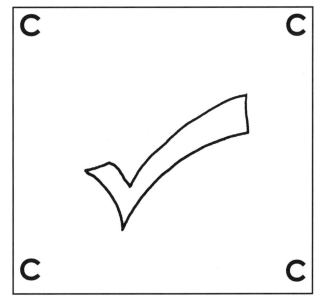

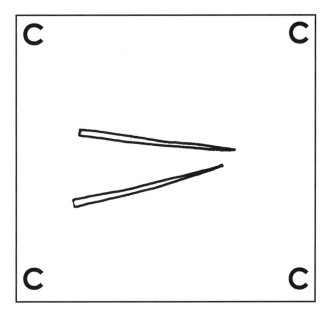

Chair, Checkmark, Chicken, Chopsticks. ***Other choices:*** *Chain, Chariot, Cheetah, Cherry, Chimney, Chimp, Chin, Chipmunk, Chocolate Chip.*

C

Ch

Cher

Letter links for names that begin with **Ch (sounds like /sh/)**

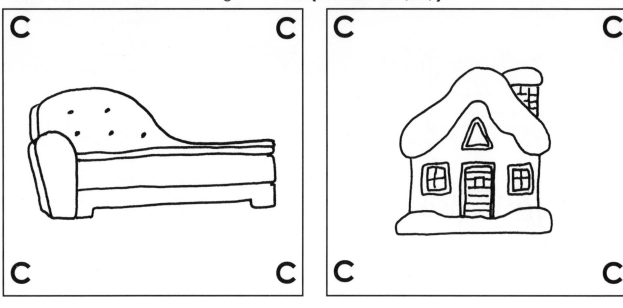

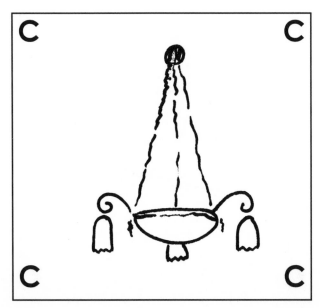

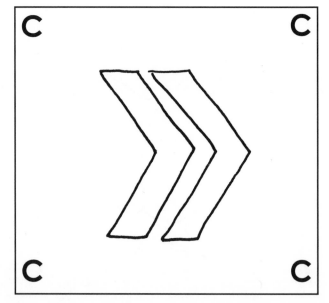

Chaise lounge, Chalet, Chandelier, Chevron. ***Other choices:*** *Chateau, Chef, Chemise.*

C

CI

Claire

Letter links for names that begin with **Cl**

Climber, Clock, Clothespin, Cloud. **Other choices:** *Clam, Clamp, Clarinet, Claw, Cloak, Clown.*

C

Chr/Cr

Sample nametag

Chris (or) Craig

Letter links for names that begin with **Chr/Cr**

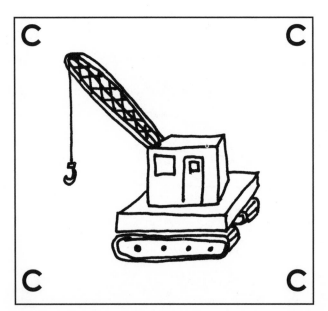

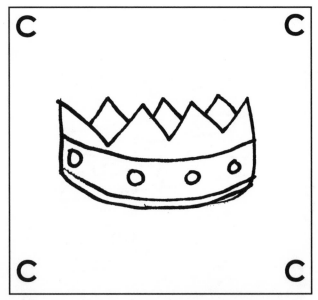

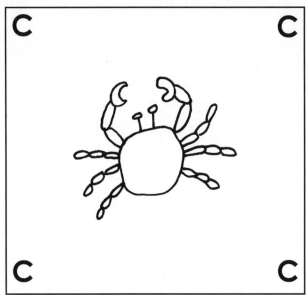

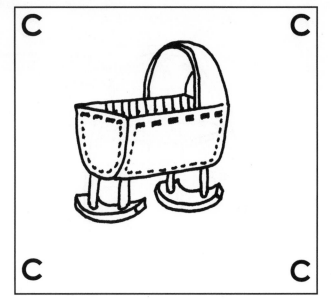

Crab, Cradle, Crane, Crown. **Other choices:** *Chrysalis, Chrysanthemum, Cracker, Creel, Crescent, Crib, Cricket, Crocodile.*

Sample nametag

D

| D | **Dewan** |

Letter links for names that begin with **D**

Dog, Door, Duck, Dump truck. ***Other choices:*** *Deer, Doll, Dolphin.*

D
Dr

Drew

Letter links for names that begin with **Dr**

D 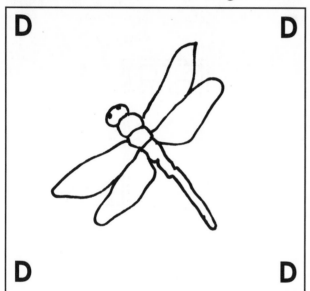 D
D D

D  D
D D

D 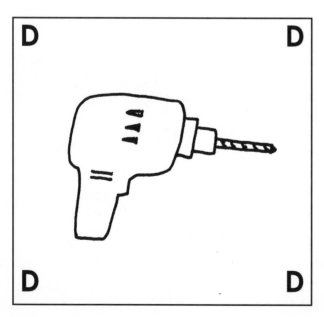 D
D D

D  D
D D

Dragonfly, Dress, Drill, Drum. **Other choices:** Dragon, Drop, Dropper.

E

Short E

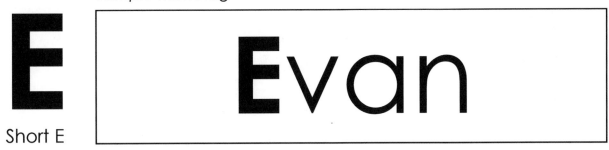

Evan

Letter links for names that begin with **short E**

Egg, Elephant, Elf, Envelope. **Other choices:** *Eggplant, Eggshell, Elk, Engine.*

E

Long E

Eva

Letter links for names that begin with **long E**

Eagle, Easel, Emu, Evening gown. **Other choices:** *Ear, Eel, Egret.*

E

Ei

Eileen

Letter links for names that begin with **Ei (sounds like long I)**

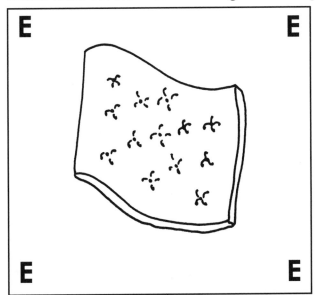

Eiderdown, Eider duck, Eiffel Tower.

E

Er

Sample nametag

Ernest

Letter links for names that begin with an **Er**

Ermine, erne.

Sample nametag

E
Eu

E Eugene

Letter links for names that begin with **Eu (sounds like /yoo/)**

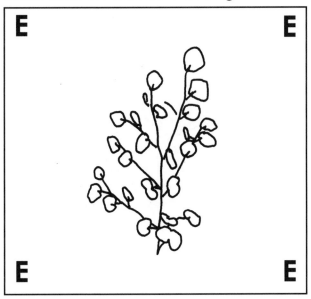

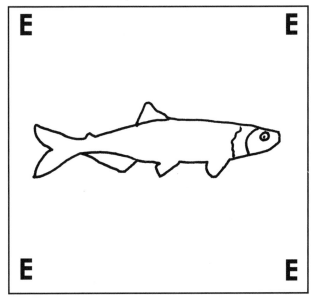

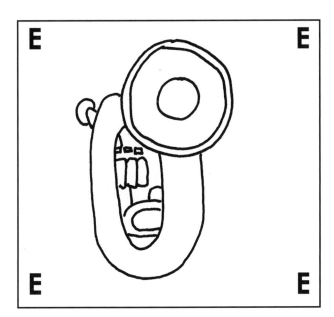

Eucalyptus, Eulachon (candlefish), Euphonium (similar to tuba), Euro (Australian name for kangaroo). **Other choices:** *Euphorbia (type of plant).*

F

Sample nametag

Fergus

Letter links for names that begin with **F**

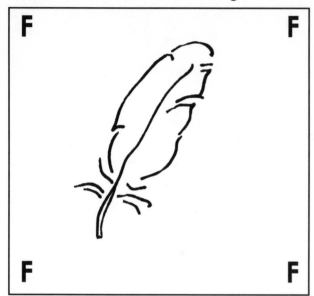

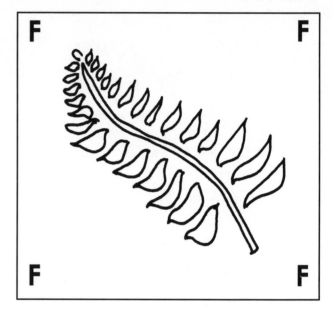

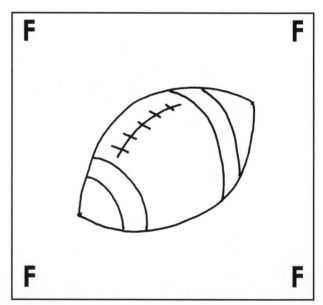

Feather, Fern, Fire truck, Football. **Other choices:** *Fan, Faucet, Fish, Foot, Fox.*

F

Fl

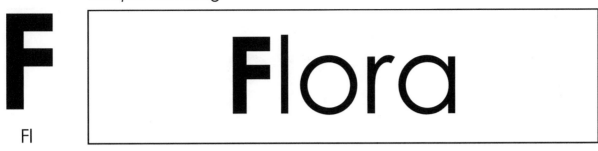

Letter links for names that begin with **Fl**

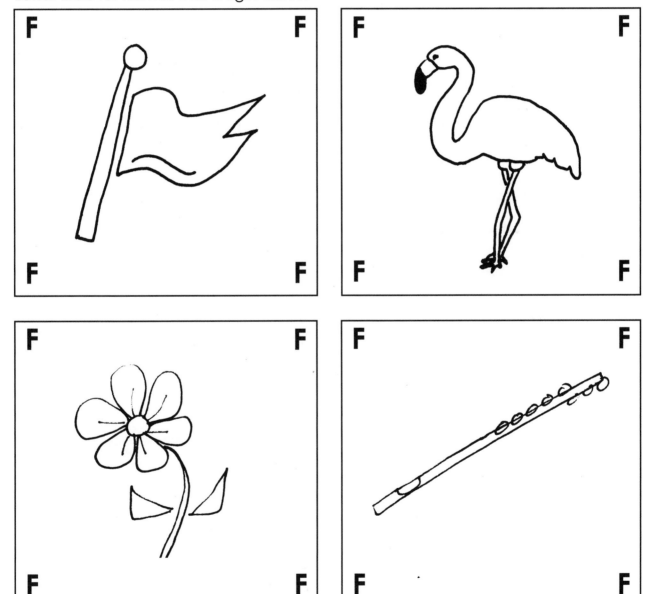

Flag, Flamingo, Flower, Flute. **Other choices:** *Flagpole, Flame, Flapjack, Flashlight, Flatcar, Fleur-de-lis, Flounder, Flying saucer.*

F

Fr

Frieda

Letter links for names that begin with **Fr**

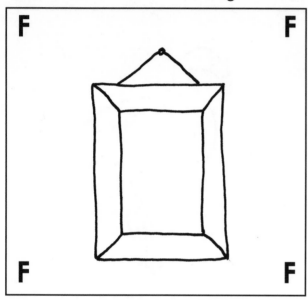

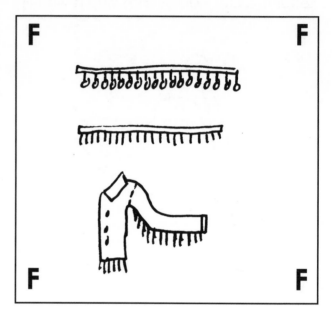

Frame, Fringe, Frog, Frying pan. **Other choices:** *Fridge, Frijole (kidney bean).*

G

Hard G

Letter links for names that begin with **hard G**

Gate, Ghost, Goat, Guitar. ***Other choices:*** *Gears, Gift, Gorilla, Gourd, Guinea pig.*

Sample nametag

G
Soft G

| G | Georgia |

Letter links for names that begin with **soft G (sounds like /j/)**

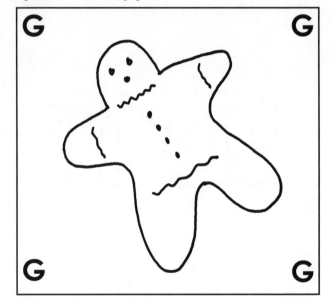

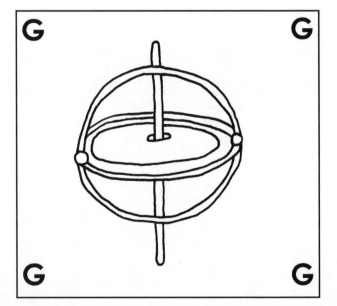

Gerbil, Gingerbread man, Giraffe, Gyroscope. **Other choices:** *Gem, Geode, Giant.*

Sample nametag

G

Gl

Letter links for names that begin with **Gl**

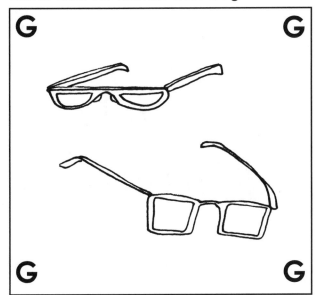

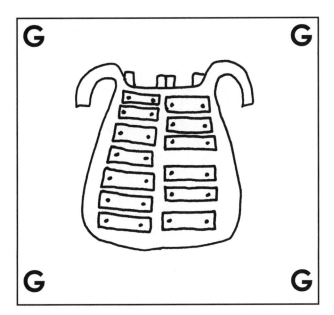

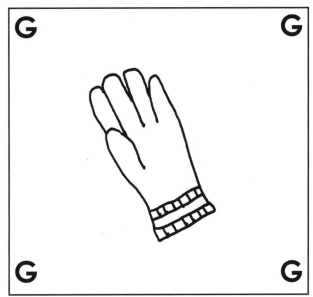

Glasses, Globe, Glockenspiel, Glove. **Other choices:** *Gladiolus, Glass.*

G

Gr

Grace

Letter links for names that begin with **Gr**

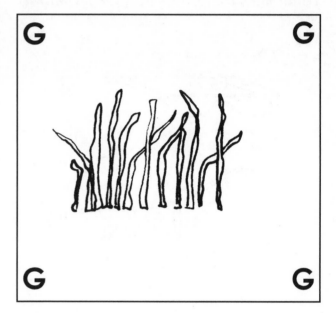

Grapes, Grass, Grasshopper, Griffin. **Other choices:** Graham cracker, Grain, Grandfather clock, Grandma, Grapefruit, Graph, Grater, Green bean, Greenhouse, Griddlecake.

H | **H**abib

Letter links for names that begin with **H**

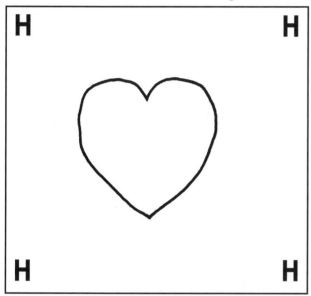

Heart, Helicopter, Horse, House. **Other choices:** *Hammer, Hand, Harmonica, Harp, Hawk, Hat, Hedgehog, Hippo, Hose.*

Iggy

Short I

Letter links for names that begin with **short I**

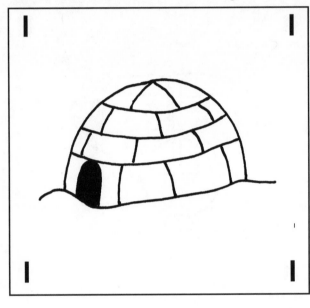

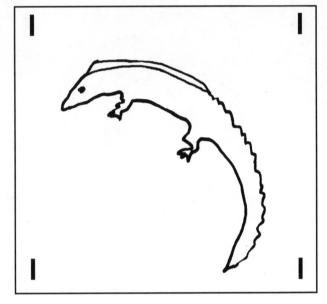

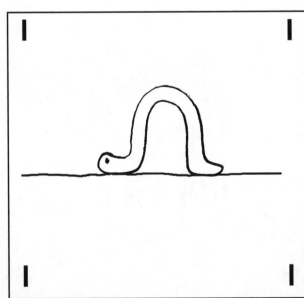

Igloo, Iguana, Inchworm, Ink. **Other choices:** *Inch.*

I

Long I

Irene

Letter links for names that begin with a **long I**

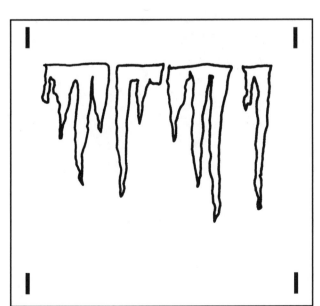

Ice-cream cone, Ice skate, Icicle, Iron. **Other choices:** *Island, Ivy.*

J

Josh

Letter links for names that begin with **J**

J	J	J	J

J	J	J	J

J	J	J	J
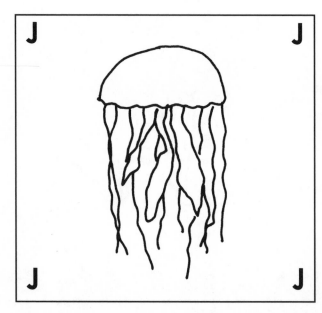			
J	J	J	J

Jack-in-the-box, Jack-o'-lantern, Jellyfish, Juggler. **Other choices:** *Jacket, Jar, Jet, Jug.*

Sample nametag

K | **K**eeya

Letter links for names that begin with **K**

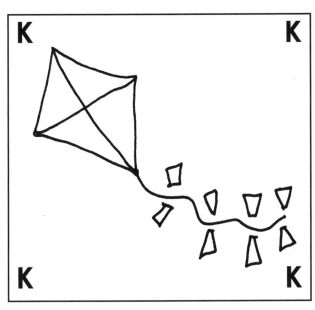

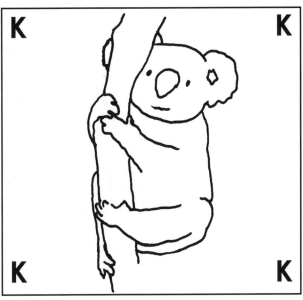

Kangaroo, Key, Kite, Koala. **Other choices:** *Kayak, Kettle, Kettledrum, King, Kiwi.*

K

Kr

K**rystal**

Letter links for names that begin with **Kr**

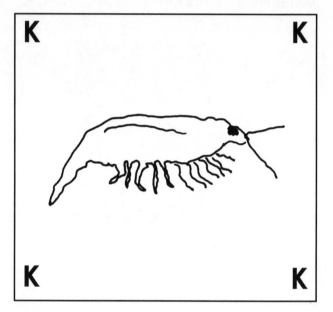

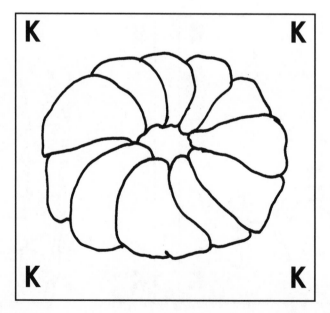

Kraken (sea monster), Krill (small marine crustaceans), Kruller (cruller).
Other choices: *Kraal (enclosure for cattle).*

L

Liam

Letter links for names that begin with **L**

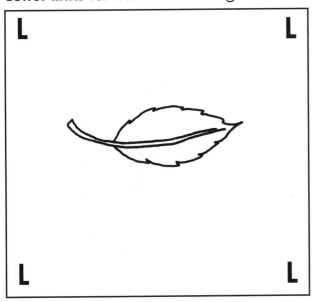

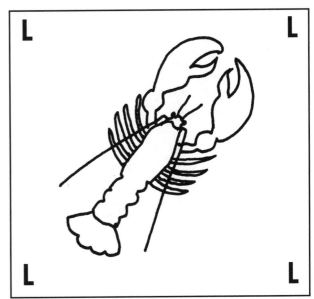

Leaf, Lighthouse, Lion, Lobster. **Other choices:** *Ladle, Ladybug, Lamb, Lamp, Lasso, Lei, Lemon, Lock.*

Sample nametag

M | Miyoko

Letter links for names that begin with **M**

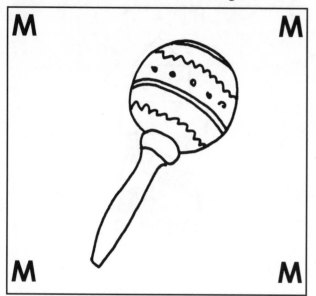

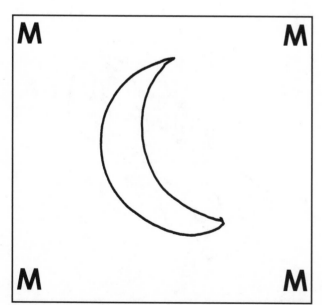

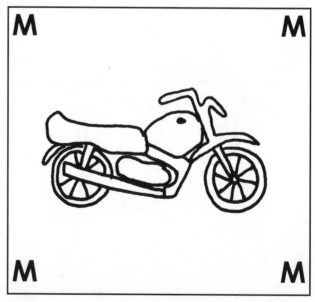

Maraca, Mitten, Moon, Motorcycle. **Other choices:** *Magnet, Mask, Mermaid, Monkey, Mop, Moose, Mountain, Mouse, Mouth, Mustache.*

Sample nametag

N | # Nick

Letter links for names that begin with **N**

N   N
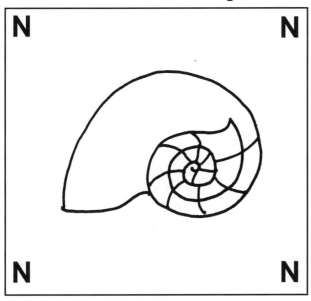
N   N

N   N
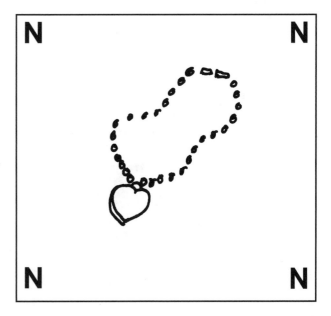
N   N

N   N
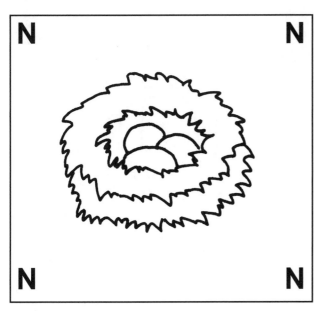
N   N

N   N

N   N

Nautilus, Necklace, Nest, Newspaper. **Other choices:** *Nail, Needle, Nose, Nurse, Nut.*

O

Short O

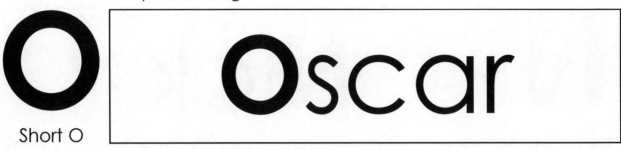

Oscar

Letter links for names that begin with a **short O**

Octopus, Ostrich, Otter, Owl. **Other choices:** *Ocarina, Olive, Ox.*

 **O**

Long O

Okalani

Letter links for names that begin with a **long O**

Oatmeal, Oboe, Ocean, Overalls. **Other choices:** *Opal, Osage orange.*

O

Or

O

Letter links for names that begin with an **Or**

Orangutan, Orca, Ornament, Oryx. **Other choices:** *Orange, Orb, Orchard, Orchestra, Orchid, Organ, Organ grinder, Organ-pipe cactus, Oriole.*

Sample nametag

P

Letter links for names that begin with **P**

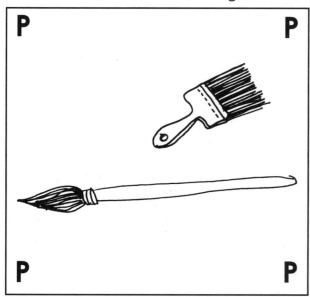

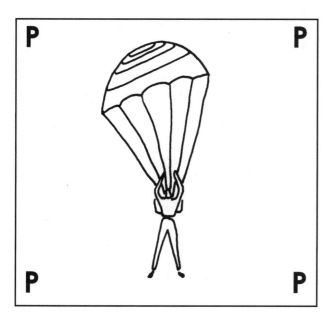

Paintbrush, Palm tree, Parachute, Penguin. ***Other choices:*** *Pagoda, Pan, Panda, Pants, Parrot, Peacock, Peanut, Pea pod, Pelican, Pie, Pig, Pineapple, Pocket, Pogo stick.*

P

Ph

Sample nametag

Philip

Letter links for names that begin with **Ph (sounds like /f/)**

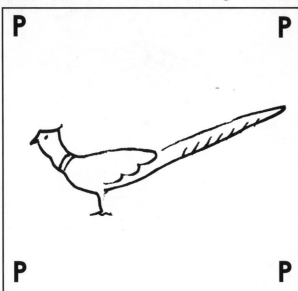

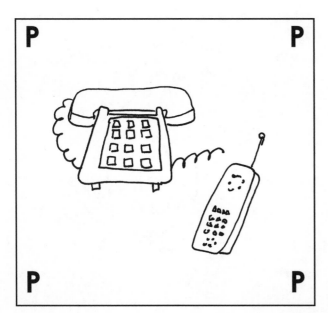

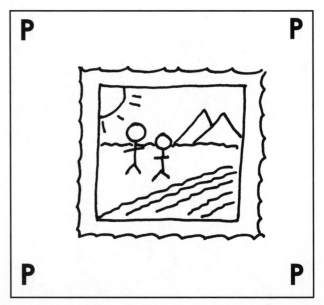

Pheasant, Phoenix, Phone, Photo. ***Other choices:*** *Phone booth, Photographer.*

74   Letter Links

P

PI

Plato

Letter links for names that begin with **PI**

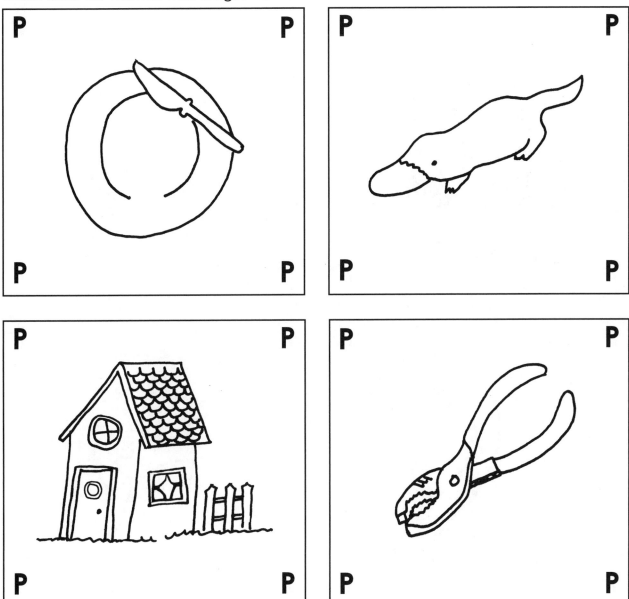

Plate, Platypus, Playhouse, Pliers. **Other choices:** *Place mat, Plane (tool),
Playing card, Playpen, Plow, Plug, Plum, Plumb bob, Plume.*

P

Pr

Sample nametag

Prya

Letter links for names that begin with **Pr**

P P 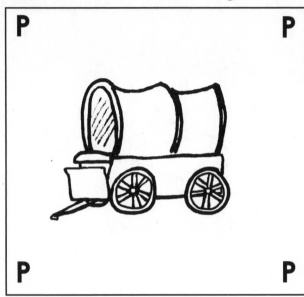 P P	P P 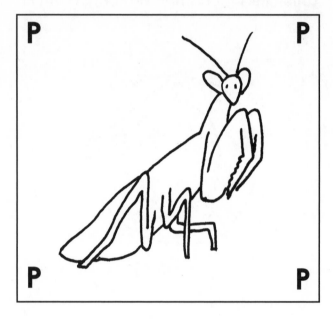 P P
P P 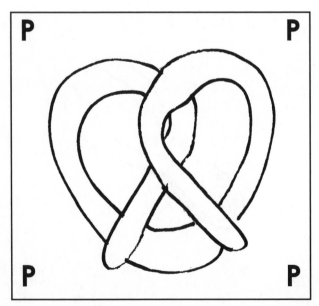 P P	P P 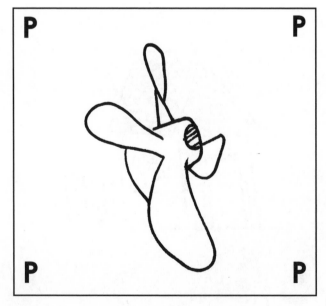 P P

Prairie schooner, Praying mantis, Pretzel, Propeller. **Other choices:** *Prairie dog, Prawn, Printer, Prism, Proboscis, Profile.*

Quinta

Letter links for names that begin with **Q**

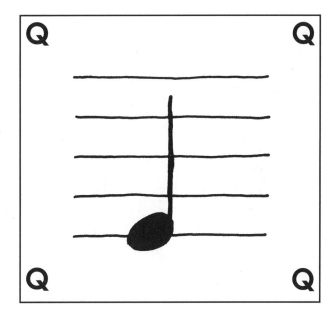

Quail, Quarter note, Queen, Quilt. **Other choices:** *Quarter (coin), Question mark, Quotation marks, Quiver.*

R

Rob

Letter links for names that begin with **R**

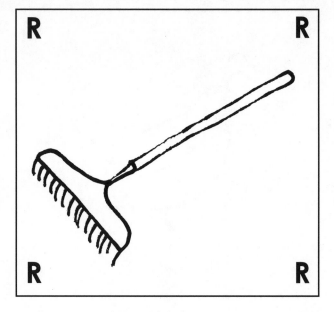

Rabbit, Rake, Rhinoceros, Robot. **Other choices:** *Raccoon, Rattlesnake, Ribbon, Ring, Rock, Rocking chair, Rocking horse, Roller blade.*

Sample nametag

S

| **S** ara |

Letter links for names that begin with **S**

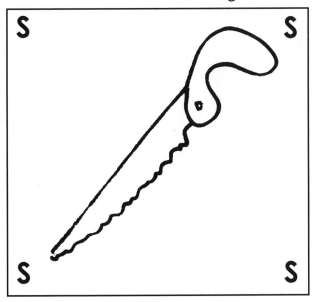

Saw, Scissors, Seal, Sun. **Other choices:** *Sail boat, Sand dollar, Sea horse, Seesaw, Sink, Soap, Sock.*

Sample nametag

Scott

Sc

Letter links for names that begin with **Sc**

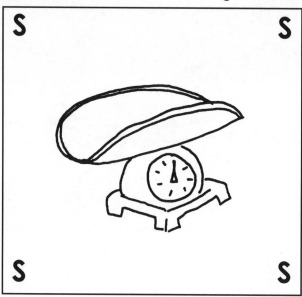

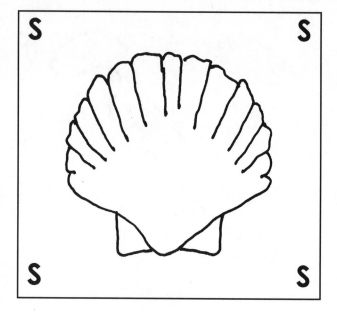

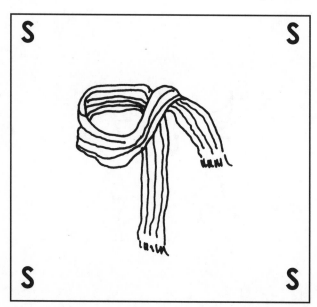

Scale, Scallop, Scarf, Scooter. **Other choices:** *Scarecrow, School, Schooner, Scoop, Scorpion.*

S

Sh

| **S**hemeka |

Letter links for names that begin with **Sh**

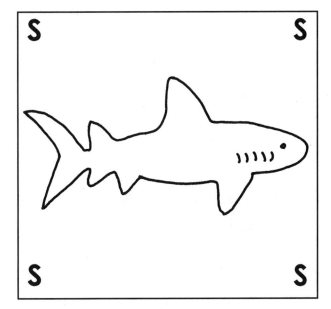

Shamrock, Shark, Shield, Shovel. **Other choices:** *Sheep, Shell, Ship, Shirt.*

S
Sk

Sample nametag

Skye

Letter links for names that begin with **Sk**

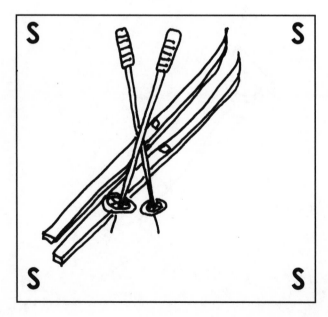

Skate, Skateboard, Skis, Skunk. **Other choices:** *Skeleton, Skink, Skirt.*

Sample nametag

S
SI

Slade

Letter links for names that begin with **Sl**

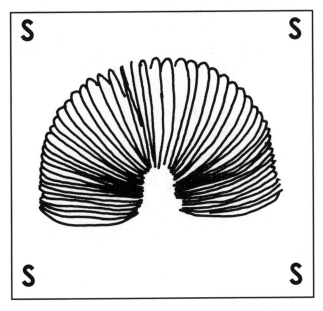

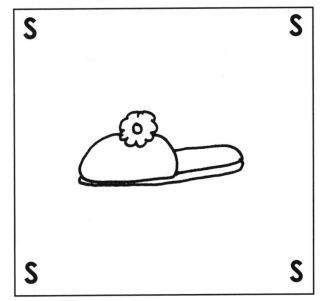

Sled, Slide, Slinky, Slipper. **Other choices:** *Sleeve, Sleigh.*

Sample nametag

Snolly

Letter links for names that begin with **Sn**

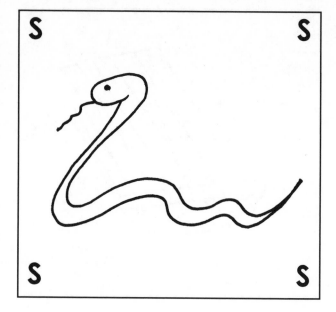

Snail, Snake, Snare drum, Snowflake. ***Other choices:*** Snowman, Snowplow, *Snowshoe.*

S

Sp

Spencer

Letter links for names that begin with **Sp**

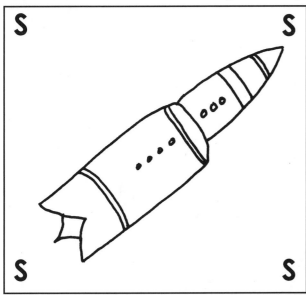

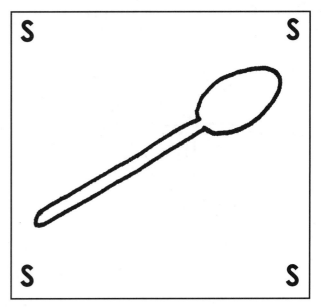

Spaceship, Spatula, Spider, Spoon. **Other choices:** *Spindle, Spinning wheel, Sponge, Spool.*

S

St

Stefan

Letter links for names that begin with **St**

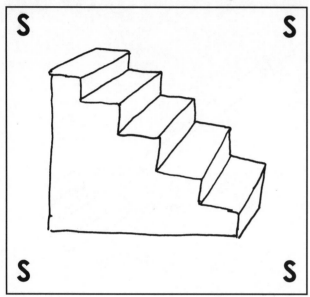

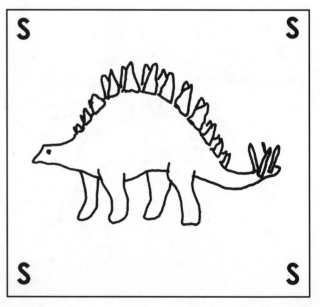

Stairs, Star, Steam shovel, Stegosaurus. **Other choices:** Steeple, Stool, Stove, Strawberry, Stump.

S
Sw

| **S**weeny |

Letter links for names that begin with **Sw**

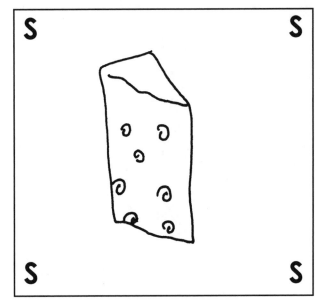

Swan, Swimmer, Swing, Swiss cheese. ***Other choices:*** *Sweater, Switch.*

T

Sample nametag

Ted

Letter links for names that begin with **T**

Tambourine, Teapot, Tepee, Turtle. **Other choices:** *Target, Teardrop, Tent, Tiger, Tire, Toboggan, Toe, Tooth, Torch, Turkey, Tyrannosaurus.*

T
Th

Sample nametag

Theo

Letter links for names that begin with **Th**

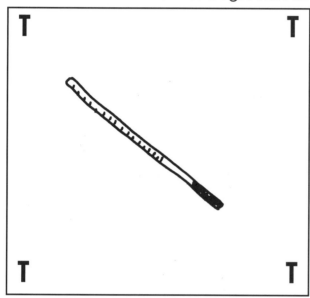

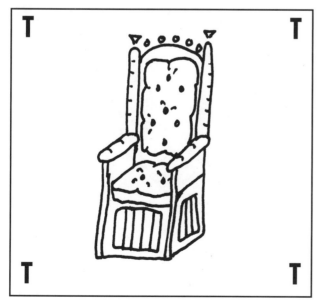

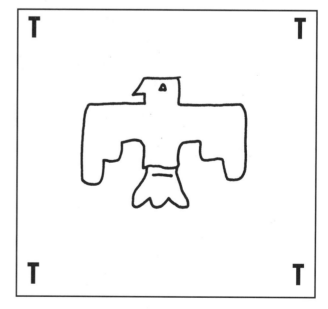

Thermometer, Thread, Throne, Thunderbird. **Other choices:** Thimble, Thistle, Thorn, Thumb.

Nametags and Letter Links **89**

T

Tr

Travis

Letter links for names that begin with **Tr**

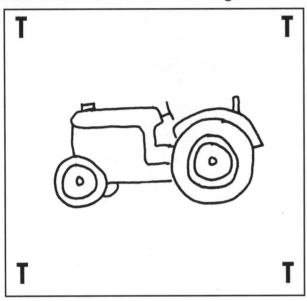

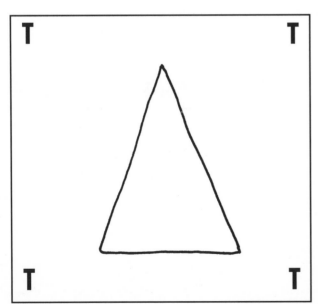

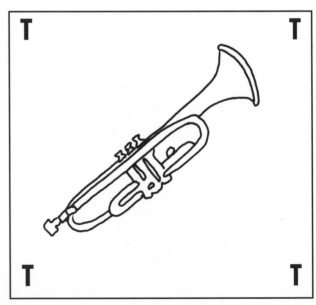

Tractor, Tree, Triangle, Trumpet. **Other choices:** *Train, Trampoline, Trapezoid, Travois, Triceratops, Tricycle, Truck, Trunk.*

U

U

Ukiah

Letter links for names that begin with **U (sounds like /yōo/)**

Unicorn, Unicycle.

U

Short U

Umberto

Letter links for names that begin with a **short U**

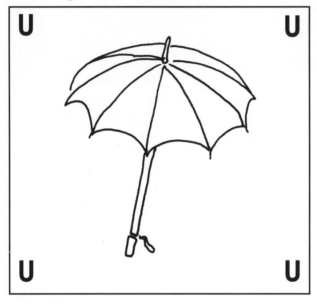

Umbrella, Undershirt.

U

Ur

Ursula

Letter links for names that begin with **Ur**

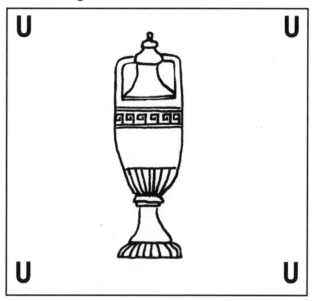

Urn.

V

Sample nametag

Vinnie

Letter links for names that begin with **V**

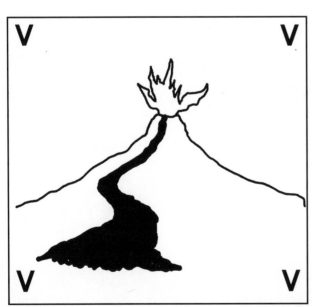

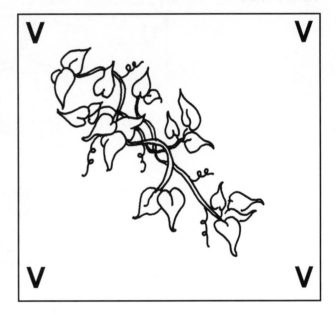

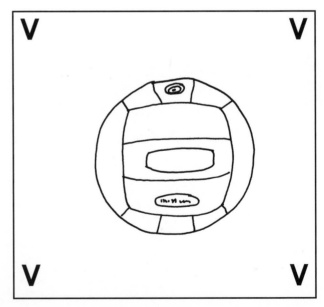

Van, Vine, Volcano, Volleyball. **Other choices:** *Vacuum cleaner, Valentine, Vase, Vest, Violin, Vise.*

W

Will

Letter links for names that begin with **W**

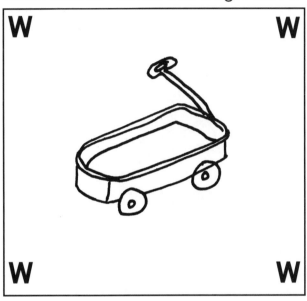

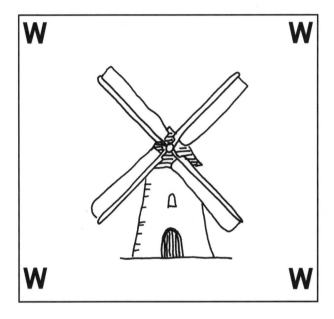

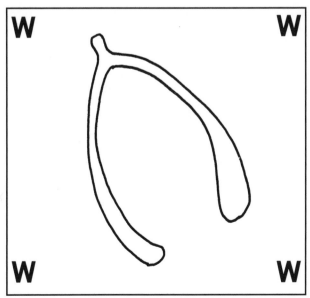

Wagon, Windmill, Window, Wishbone. **Other choices:** *Walrus, Wand, Watch, Waterfall, Watermelon, Weather vane, Web, Well, Windsock, worm.*

W

Wh

Whitney

Letter links for names that begin with **Wh**

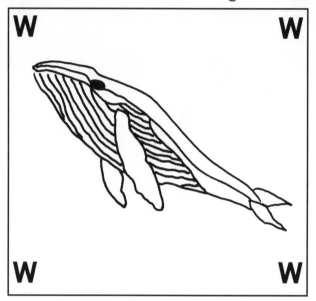

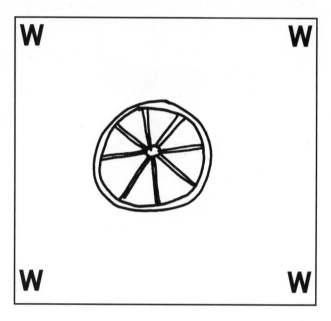

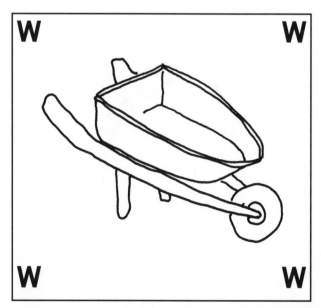

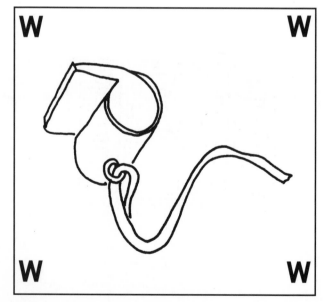

Whale, Wheel, Wheelbarrow, Whistle. **Other choices:** *Whiffle ball.*

X

Xena

Letter links for names that begin with **X (sounds like /z/)**

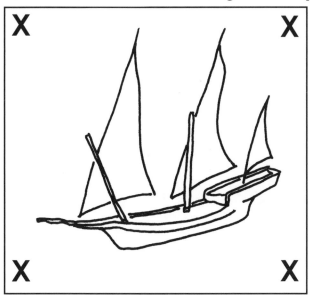

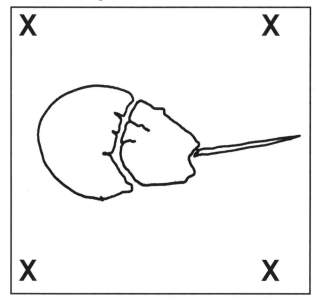

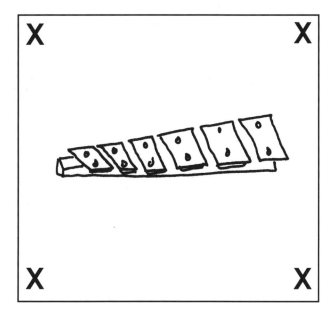

Xebec, Xiphosuran (horsehoe crab), Xylophone.

Y

Sample nametag

Yuri

Letter links for names that begin with **Y**

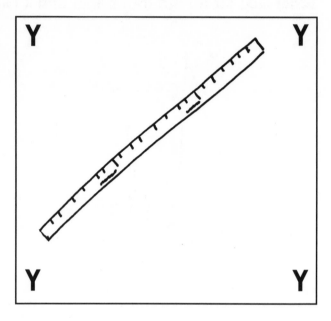

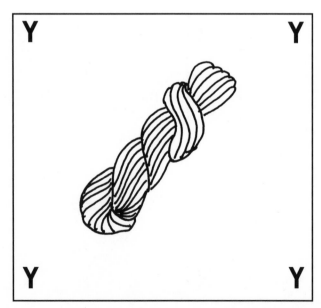

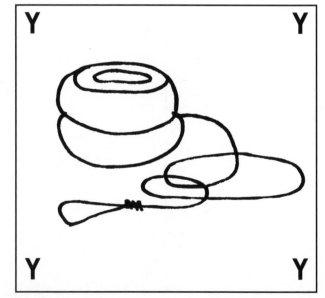

Yak, Yardstick, Yarn, Yoyo. **Other choices:** *Yam, Yogurt, Yolk.*

Z | **Z**ara

Letter links for names that begin with **Z**

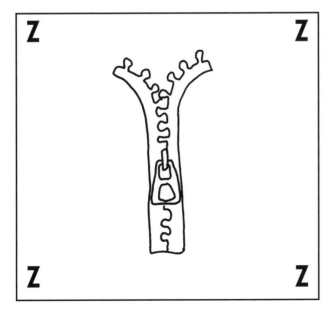

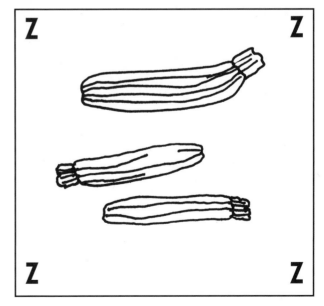

Zebra, Zigzag, Zipper, Zucchini. **Other choices:** Zero, Zoo.

About the Authors

Dr. Andrea DeBruin-Parecki, Director of the High/Scope Early Childhood Reading Institute, is nationally recognized for her work in the field of family literacy. She has developed an authentic assessment for evaluating adult/child interactive reading—the Adult/Child Interactive Reading Inventory. This instrument is now being used nationally. She also has expertise in the areas of emergent literacy, literacy within at-risk and minority populations, the motivation of at-risk populations, and the formation of intercultural friendships through literacy activities. Her work related to the psychological issues of teaching practices and literacy development in young children and families has been published and presented at national, regional, and state conferences. Her latest book, *Family Literacy From Theory to Practice,* is published by the International Reading Association.

Mary Hohmann, Senior Early Childhood Specialist, has been a member of the High/Scope Foundation since 1970. She has served as a High/Scope preschool teacher, trainer, curriculum developer and writer, and educational consultant in the United States, Norway, Finland, and Portugal. She is the principal author of High/Scope's preschool curriculum manual, *Educating Young Children: Active Learning Practices for Preschool and Child Care Programs,* co-author of *Tender Care*

and Early Learning: Supporting Infants and Toddlers in Child Care Settings, and author of *Fee, Fie, Phonemic Awareness: 130 Prereading Activities for Preschoolers.* She is also one of the developers of the *High/Scope Preschool Child Observation Record* and the *High/Scope Infant-Toddler Child Observation Record,* assessment tools used in early childhood settings worldwide.

Related High/Scope® Resources

Preschool Reading

Fee, Fie, Phonemic Awareness— 130 Prereading Activities for Preschoolers

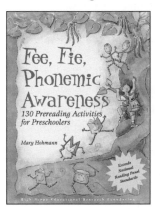

Endorsed by the High/Scope Early Childhood Reading Institute, this book focuses on phonemic awareness— the ability to recognize the smallest sound units that make up words—identified by reading experts as an essential skill that prepares children for reading. The 130 activities are suitable for small-group learning in preschools, prekindergarten programs, Head Start programs, child care centers, and home-based programs. The activities are based on the latest scientific evidence about what children need to become confident and successful readers and writers. They also reflect the research-based, classroom-tested, and internationally recognized teaching strategies of the High/Scope early childhood approach. The book offers more than enough activities to meet the standard of 20 hours of phonemic awareness practice recommended for preschoolers by the National Reading Panel and endorsed by the U.S. Department of Education.

BK-P1190 $25.95

M. Hohmann. Soft cover, 80 pages, photos. 1-57379-128-8

Language and Literacy

Using the ideas in this book-let, you can help preschoolers expand their conversational abilities and discover the usefulness and fun of the written word by introducing six key experiences in language and literacy. The booklet includes both a list of materials for supporting early reading and writing and a teaching strategy checklist. The colorful, informative video features adults supporting and extending children's language and literacy experiences in actual High/Scope classrooms and centers.

Book: BK-P1155 $9.95 Video: BK-P1156 $30.95
Set: BK-P1157SET $34.95

Book, soft cover, photos, 28 pages. 1-57379-097-4; Video, color, 60 min. 1-57379-098-2

Educating Young Children: Active Learning Practices for Preschool and Child Care Programs (2ⁿᵈ Ed.)

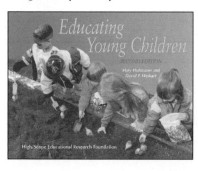

The updated chapters in this second edition of High/Scope's preschool manual include informa-tion on phonemic awareness and preschool read-ing, additional references, the latest Perry Preschool research results, recent research relating to brain development, and a complete description of a consistent approach to problem solving. Written for early childhood practitioners and students, this manual presents essential strategies adults can use to make active learning a reality in their programs. Describes key compo-nents of the adult's role: planning the physical setting and establishing a consistent daily routine; creating a positive social climate; and using High/Scope's 58 "key experiences" in child development to understand and support young children. Other topics include family involvement, daily team planning, interest areas, appropriate materials, the plan-do-review process, and small- and large-group times. Offers numerous anecdotes, photographs, illustrations, real-life scenarios, and practical suggestions for adults. Reflects High/Scope's current research findings and over 30 years of experience.

BK-P1178 $42.95

M. Hohmann & D. P. Weikart. Soft cover, Lavishly illustrated, 560 pages. 1-57379-104-0

Related High/Scope® Resources

Preschool Reading

Helping Your Preschool Child Become a Reader—Ideas for Parents

This handy booklet gives you many simple, enjoyable ideas for using everyday experiences to help your child get ready to read. By including a wide variety of language and print experiences in your family routines, you can prepare your child not only to be successful at reading and writing but also to enjoy using these skills for a lifetime!

BK-F1059 $4.95

A. S. Epstein. Soft cover, 5¹/₂" x 8¹/₂", 48 pages, photos. 1-57379-126-1

You & Your Child Parent Newsletter Series

Practical child development information written by High/Scope staff in clear, concise language for parents. Each newsletter addresses a specific topic of interest to parents and includes helpful support strategies they can use at home. The complete *You & Your Child* series contains enough material for an entire year of monthly parent newsletters for your program!

The complete *You & Your Child* package contains 12 sets of newsletters (each set includes 25 newsletters), plus 25 customized pocket folders to hold the newsletters, and 400 attractively designed pages with room for sites to imprint news and notes about their program. These pages can be inserted in the newsletters as they are distributed. The 4-page newsletters are 3-hole-drilled for easy insertion in the customized folder provided.

Each newsletter contains photos, captions, and content that is easy to understand and read and that covers topics important to parents:

Young Children and Reading	BK-P1163-17
Young Children and Writing	BK-P1163-18
Young Children and Mathematics	BK-P1163-21
Young Children and Art	BK-P1163-16
Young Children and Dramatic Play	BK-P1163-11
Young Children and Music	BK-P1163-22
Young Children and Movement	BK-P1163-20
Young Children as Family Members	BK-P1163-19
Young Children as Communicators	BK-P1163-14
Young Children as Decision Makers	BK-P1163-12
Young Children as Challengers	BK-P1163-15
Young Children as Problem Solvers	BK-P1163-13

Complete Newsletter Package

Sets of 25 newsletters, 25 customized pocket folders, and 400 custom pages for you to imprint with local news.

BK-P1167SET $299.95
Special offer, just $254.95, save $45!

Individual Components:

25 copies of one newsletter
See the list above for code numbers **$12.95**

25 copies each of all 12 newsletters
BK-P1163 $144.95
Special offer, just $130.95, save $14!

25 customized pocket folders
BK-P1164 $139.95
Special offer, just $84.95, save $55!

400 already designed pages
For sites to use for presenting their own information and inserting in each newsletter distributed.
BK-P1165 $65.95
Special offer, just $39.95, save $26!

Six Posters on Young Children and Reading

These colorful and attractive posters will help educators and parents recognize and support important literacy concepts as they interact with and care for young children. *Titles: What Is Preschool Reading?, What Is Preschool Writing?, Support Child Talk!, Hearing the Sounds That Make Up Words, Supporting Children's Storytelling, 12 Things Parents Can Do to Help Their Preschool Child Become a Reader.*

BK-P1189 $17.95

High/Scope Early Childhood Reading Institute. Each poster is 11" x 17", full color, and contains an attractive photo. 1-57379-127-X

To order these or any other High/Scope® products, contact High/Scope® Press: phone (800)40-PRESS fax (800)442-4FAX
To see a full listing of High/Scope® products, visit our Web site: *www.highscope.org*

Related High/Scope® Resources

Elementary Reading

Literature-Based Workshops for Mathematics—Ideas for Active Learning, Grades K–2

Discover how to use high-quality children's literature—a treasure-trove of math concepts—to plan exciting small-group workshops in mathematics for young children. Each of the six sets of field-tested workshops is built around storybooks children love and focuses on a specific aspect of numeracy: shapes, counting, seriation, addition, money, and measurement. An introductory section explains the High Scope active learning small-group workshop process and provides tips on planning successful workshop experiences. Each workshop plan is geared to specific High/ Scope key experiences in mathematics and other important content areas. Includes student instruction cards and other handouts. To order the storybooks associated with the workshops, visit our online store: *www.highscope.org/welcome.asp.*

BK-E3039 $34.95

K. Morrison, T. Dittrich, & J. Claridge. Soft cover, illustrated, handouts, 224 pages. 1-57379-167-9

Literature-Based Workshops for Language Arts—Ideas for Active Learning, Grades K–2

Looking for meaningful ways to integrate high-quality children's literature into your language arts curriculum? This delightfully illustrated book provides a host of exciting small-group workshops for children in kindergarten through second grade, planned around storybooks they love. Each workshop is geared to specific High/Scope elementary key experiences and includes a description of the activity, a materials list, instructions for teachers and students, follow-up activities, and modifications for children with special needs. The workshops focus on several classic as well as new children's books, such as Where's My Teddy?, The Napping House, Monster Mama, The Z Was Zapped, the Amelia Bedelia series, and many others! To order the storybooks associated with the workshops, visit our online store: *www.highscope.org/welcome.asp.*

BK-E3017 $34.95

K. Morrison, T. Dittrich, & J. Claridge. Illustrated, soft cover, 224 pages. 1-57379-091-5

High/Scope K–2 Workshop Companion Storybooks

For your convenience, High/Scope Press has made arrangements to offer a number of the storybooks used in the workshops described in *Literature-Based Workshops for Language Arts* and *Literature-Based Workshops for Mathematics* (subject to publisher's availability). Each is offered at 15% off list price!

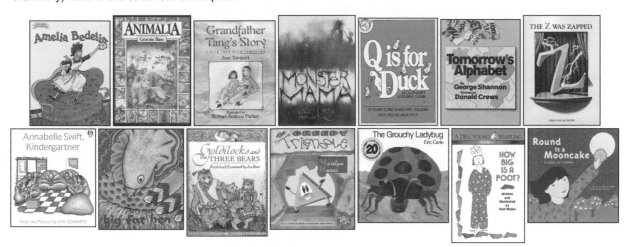

See the next page for descriptions and prices.

Related High/Scope® Resources

Elementary Reading

Language Arts Workshops

Title	Code	List Price	Our Price
ABC T-Rex	BK-EHB518	$13.00	$11.05
Amelia Bedelia	BK-EHB544	$14.99	$12.74
Amelia Bedelia and the Surprise Shower	BK-EHB546	$15.99	$13.59
Amelia Bedelia's Family Album	BK-EHB526	$15.99	$13.59
Animalia	BK-EHB565	$11.95	$11.95
Brown Bear, What Do You See?	BK-EHB161	$17.00	$14.45
Cowboy Alphabet	BK-EHB748	$14.95	$14.95
Goldilocks and the Three Bears (Brett)	BK-EHB762	$16.99	$14.44
Goldilocks and the Three Bears (Marshall)	BK-EHB569	$15.99	$13.59
Good Driving, Amelia Bedelia	BK-EHB520	$15.99	$13.59
Grandfather Tang's Story	BK-EHB558	$16.00	$13.60
Handmade Alphabet, The	BK-EHB324	$17.99	$15.29
Jolly Postman, The	BK-EHB560	$17.95	$15.26
Monster Mama	BK-EHB554	$15.99	$13.59
My Friend Bear	BK-EHB512	$16.99	$14.44
Napping House, The	BK-EHB110	$16.00	$13.60
Play Ball, Amelia Bedelia	BK-EHB548	$15.99	$13.59
Q Is for Duck	BK-EPB408	$6.95	$5.91
Ragged Bear	BK-EPB402	$6.95	$5.91
Tomorrow's Alphabet	BK-EHB540	$16.99	$14.44
Where's My Teddy?	BK-EHB516	$16.99	$14.44
Z Was Zapped, The	BK-EHB550	$17.99	$15.29
Language Arts Workshops Set	BK-EHB10	$335.62	$289.30

Mathematics Workshops

Title	Code	List Price	Our Price
Alexander, Who Used to Be Rich Last Sunday	BK-EHB776	$16.00	$13.60
Anabelle Swift, Kindergartner	BK-EPB420	$6.95	$5.91
Anno's Counting Book	BK-EHB500	$16.99	$14.44
Benny's Pennies	BK-EPB346	$6.99	$5.94
Big Fat Hen	BK-PHB115	$16.00	$13.60
A Chair for My Mother	BK-EHB494	$15.99	$13.59
Each Orange Had 8 Slices	BK-EHB380	$15.99	$13.59
The Fattest, Tallest, Biggest Snowman Ever	BK-EPB394	$3.99	$3.39
Goldilocks and the Three Bears	BK-EHB762	$16.99	$14.44
The Greedy Triangle	BK-EHB390	$15.95	$13.56
The Grouchy Ladybug	BK-EHB775	$16.99	$14.44
How Big Is a Foot?	BK-EPB382	$3.99	$3.39
How Many Teeth?	BK-EPB334	$4.99	$4.24
The Icky Bug Counting Book	BK-EHB369	$16.95	$16.95
Inch by Inch	BK-EPB479	$5.99	$5.09
Is a Blue Whale the Biggest Thing There Is?	BK-EHB355	$13.95	$13.95
Me and the Measure of Things	BK-EHB844	$12.95	$11.01
Pigs Will Be Pigs	BK-EHB431	$15.00	$12.75
Round Is a Mooncake: A Book About Shapes	BK-EHB436	$13.95	$11.86
Shapes, Shapes, Shapes	BK-EHB381	$15.99	$13.59
Ten Black Dots	BK-EHB117	$15.99	$13.59
12 Ways to Get to 11	BK-EPB109	$6.99	$5.94
The Very Hungry Caterpillar	BK-PHB163	$19.99	$16.99
Mathematics Workshops Set	BK-EHB20	$295.56	$255.85

All books subject to publisher's availability.

Visit High/Scope's online store, *www.highscope.org/welcome.asp*, for details.

To order these or any other High/Scope® products, contact High/Scope® Press: phone (800)40-PRESS fax (800)442-4FAX

To see a full listing of High/Scope® products, visit our Web site: *www.highscope.org*